"The courage of this author is surpassed only by the wondrous journey of the story. From her brutal honesty to the eloquent descriptions, the reader is transported through time and space. You do not read this book; you experience the life of its words as a willing participant, a wonderful and moving saga. I thank my Higher Power for putting Linda in my life, and for this book, which has changed my life."

Peter Johns

"Fantastic! A truly historical document that may surpass other writings previously written, and possibly ever to be written, about the life of Mary Magdalene. She was a strong but loving woman well beyond what was expected of the times. Amazingly, she met the challenge of being the wife and companion to him who we know to be Jesus.

A gripping account of Magdalene's life with Jeshua ben Joseph. It brings one not only to the point of heart-wrenching tears, but becomes naturally alive within the reader as really being there; present with the Master.

Dorothy (DJ) Putz

Memories of Magdalene

By Linda M. Moore

INFINITY
PUBLISHING.COM

ISBN 0-7414-5425-4

Published by:

INFINITY
PUBLISHING.COM

1094 New DeHaven Street, Suite 100
West Conshohocken, PA 19428-2713
Info@buybooksontheweb.com
www.buybooksontheweb.com
Toll-free (877) BUY BOOK
Local Phone (610) 941-9999
Fax (610) 941-9959

Printed in the United States of America

Published May 2009

Acknowledgments

To Dick Sutphen, Jean, Jane D., and Tommie who facilitated the regressions that took me back to Palestine;

To Lynn, DJ, Tommy, Jane B., Peter, Denise and Desiree, the first readers of the manuscript who provided much appreciated feedback and encouragement;

To my late brother, Paul Cline, and his wife Arlene, who believed in me from the start;

To my beloved husband Chuck and my children, Jennifer, Chris, Wendy, and Emily, who listened and "hung in there" with me through all my questions, doubts and tears, and gently pushed me to complete this part of my mission;

And above all, to Archangel Michael, Jeshua, and Lord Sananda, whose love, gentle humor, and unfailing eternal patience gave me the keys that unlocked Palestine for me.

My undying love and gratitude to you all!

Memories of Magdalene

Chapter 1

I remember Palestine. I remember the beauty of the river Jordan in the spring lined with trees and lush green grass. I remember the songs of the birds as they flitted from branch to branch and took to the air in circles of feathers and chirping cries. I remember the warmth of the sun on my skin and the way the droning of the insects lent a lazy feeling to the warm afternoon. I remember the gentle breezes that stirred the treetops and softly blew my long hair about my face.

Yes, I remember Palestine.

I am not alone in this, for there are many of us on the planet at this time who have very vivid memories of the dusty roads of the countryside, the presence of Roman soldiers everywhere, and the tensions of a land occupied by a hostile force with an even more hostile Jewish puppet king.

Most of all, I remember shoulder length dark brown hair, large but gentle hands, and the deepest and clearest blue eyes that I have seen in any lifetime. I remember the intellect, the wisdom that poured forth from him, the timbre of his voice as he spoke the truth whether to one or to many. I recall the way he playfully growled as he chased the children in play and his loving concern as he listened to those asking for his help. I recall his joyful laugh and he laughed often. I remember his gentleness with the frail and the old, his strength and integrity, and the righteous anger that burst forth infrequently, mostly at the injustices of the political world.

Above all, I remember his warm hand on my cheek, the love in his eyes as he gazed into mine with a look that went right through my soul. I remember his voice, soft and deep as he spoke to me.

"Ah, my Beloved, my Magdalene."

Yes, I remember Jeshua. The warmth of his love and the reality of our love and the mission we embarked upon have stayed with me these two thousand years no matter in what lifetime or circumstances I found myself. I do not know if I have had the depth of recall of that time in other lifetimes that I do in this one, but I know that I have not lived one time in all the years since Palestine when I did not yearn for his presence and mourn his absence from my side.

How did I know of the lifetime? How did the details filter through my memories and become the crystal clear picture that lives within my heart? It all started when I was but a child, in the postwar 1950's of middle class America.

I have been drawn to the Palestine story all my life on a deep soul level. I can remember sitting in church gazing up at the portrait of Jesus as the Good Shepherd behind the altar and being lost in his eyes. I felt he was looking directly at me and had the feeling that there was something I was supposed to remember. Attending Lutheran/Missouri Synod parochial school for the first eight years of my academic life gave me a good background in the Christian Bible and the beliefs and teachings of the church. I listened to the stories from the Bible as read and interpreted by my teachers and the pastor and knew that there was a kernel of the truth, but the real truth, the underlying truth of the story that I needed to have confirmed for me, was never spoken. The Bible as written and selected by the church for reading by the masses did not contain the truth that I longed to find. I had no idea what it was that I needed to find, but I knew instinctively that I would not find it in organized religion.

A classmate threw the charge of "heretic" at me when I was in the sixth grade and began asking questions, sometimes probing questions, that could not be answered by the adults in charge who were supposed to know all the answers. An example was the conversation I had with the pastor during catechism class. I asked if the seven days of creation were the same twenty-four hour days that we currently use. He answered, "Of course!" which made no sense to me. How could anyone know how God keeps track of time, if S/He does? When I voiced that concern, he told me, "Because the Bible says so." I knew there was no point in trying to find any open minds in that closed environment.

I can also remember hearing the story of Mary Magdalene for the first time. My teacher ascribed to her the role of the harlot caught in adultery and taken to be stoned. I actually bristled at that assumption and knew in the depths of my soul that the entire story was not as reported. My reaction made no sense to me at the time and would not for another 35 years.

As I matured, I started looking for answers in non-traditional places. I discovered the works of Arthur Ford, Edgar Cayce and Ruth Montgomery and recognized for the first time the Universal truths that I had always carried within my heart and soul but been unable to articulate. I read and studied all the esoteric and metaphysical information I could find for the next 25 years, accepting the information that resonated within and either rejecting outright or withholding judgment on information that did not feel quite right.

As my husband and I raised our family through the years, we discussed all the information we were reading and discovering and our children grew up with many of the beliefs and knowledge that we had worked so hard to discover. There were signs along the way that pointed me to the memories that would emerge, signs that I recognized only in hindsight.

When the movie version of "Jesus Christ Superstar" hit the theaters, my husband and I went to see it. We saw through the theatrics of the machine guns and tanks to the emotions and the underlying drama. The scene in the garden of Gethsemane, where Jesus climbed the mountain asking for the cup to be taken from him and seeing paintings through the centuries of the crucifixion, was the emotional turning point for me. I sat with my arms folded tightly across my solar plexus trying desperately to maintain control, nearly giving in to the hysterics that threatened to overwhelm me. I had no earthly idea where all that emotion came from; I just knew that I could not bear to see the scenes before me. A huge raw place within my heart and soul was torn and bleeding and the weeping that was so close to the surface would have been uncontrollable if I had allowed it to manifest.

I did not discuss the strange reaction with anyone.

I attended Catholic mass with my husband's family and friends and was disturbed by the emphasis on the suffering and death, the torture and the blood of Jesus' death rather than on the positive and beautiful words and events of his life. One day, kneeling in prayer before an unusually large and gruesome replica of the crucifixion, I felt a return of the overpowering emotional reaction that I had experienced at the screening of "Superstar". I knew that I would not be able to control an outburst if that emotion returned again as strongly. That was the last time I set foot in a Catholic Church.

Why the overwhelming emotion? It made little sense to me at the time, but then, I allowed myself little time to think about it. I continued reading and studying, raising our four children, living as a Navy wife and moving from place to place every three years, and obtaining my college degree. I had so much to do and so little time in which to do it.

In 1994, we were living in Florida, where my husband retired from the Navy. Finally knowing we would not have to pull up stakes again and leave, I reached out to a group of like-minded people in a small metaphysical church and began the process of seriously looking within. I was in a New Age bookstore scanning the titles and waiting for something to grab my attention when a name caught my eye and caused my heart to skip a beat. The book was Eric Klein's "The Crystal Stair." The name was Sananda.

I had never seen the name before and had no idea that this name is the one used for Jesus on the inner etheric planes. I was compelled to buy the book and hurried home to read it. As I read the beautiful channeling of the entity that identified himself as Sananda, I knew that there was a higher purpose to my being drawn to this book other than idle curiosity. I read a page of questions and answers and got my first clue.

A participant at the channeling session asked if he had been married in Palestine. Sananda replied no. "But I knew a girl named Mary."

At that moment, I was filled with a gentle energy of warmth and love and I knew beyond a shadow of a doubt that this was a message to me, an "inside joke", if you will. At the same moment, I heard a voice to my right, yet within, that called me "Beloved of Sananda" and knew it to be true. I did not understand what it meant, but I knew it was true. I had a brief moment of clarity in which I recognized myself as the "Mary" that Sananda spoke about, but quickly denied that thought. After all, the ego asked, "Who do you think you are?" From that moment on I was on a mission to find out all I could about Sananda and his Mary and to solve the puzzle that had been put before me.

Shortly thereafter, I attended a group regression in which a small group of about twenty people was relaxed into self-hypnosis and regressed to a past life, the specifics to be chosen by the Higher Self.

* * * * *

I found myself in a rocky area beside a beautiful blue sea. The sun was shining and the warm breeze blew all around me. I was a beautiful young woman about 18 or 19 years old on my way to the marketplace. I felt feminine and powerful, filled with life and the energy of youth. I walked through the marketplace speaking and flirting with the shopkeepers, inquiring after family members, and enjoying the wonderful variety of goods displayed from near and far away places. From time to time, I would stop to touch a piece of fabric or try on a piece of jewelry. I felt that I was behaving in a way that was somewhat unusual for that time and place, but it was normal and natural for me.

Following the instructions of the facilitator, I looked down to see the sandals on my feet and the gown of pale blue that I wore. In my hand was the veil, or hair covering, that I had removed in frustration and my hair was wild and windblown, again a normal feel for me. As I looked around the marketplace trying to record as many details as I could, I sensed a group moving behind me and turned to see a handsome man of regal bearing with incredibly gentle blue eyes riding a donkey. He looked at me and smiled. The small group of people with him then surrounded him and they moved toward the city gates laughing and singing joyfully.

* * * * *

At that point the facilitator brought us back to the present and asked us to share our experiences with the rest of the group. When my turn came, I related the experience and at the end, when I described the young man on the donkey, I said, "It reminded me of the day that Jeshua and the disciples went into Jerusalem." The facilitator blanched and quickly went to the next person.

I put this whole episode in the back of my mind not knowing that the key had finally been placed in the lock to my past memories. The regression facilitator, a sensitive, had somehow recognized my soul signature and had tuned in briefly during my regression using her empathic and intuitive powers to "see" what I had been viewing. She had been given the name of the identity by her spiritual guides but did not want to address it with me before I was ready to know, nor did she want to address it in a public forum. So the incident was just a pleasant regression that was interesting to think about but of no huge importance. The seed to remember, however, had been planted.

In my readings about Sananda, I discovered that he and Jeshua were considered to be one and the same, so the fascination I had always held with that Palestine life of the one known as Jesus of Nazareth took on a new meaning. It was at this time that I became increasingly curious about the woman of that time known as Mary Magdalene. The newer writings, based on research, countered the traditional view held by the Catholic Church that referred to her as the harlot caught in the act of adultery in the New Testament story. Mary's status as harlot appeared to be an invention of the early church to counter the fact that she, not Peter, was the actual first apostle and witness to the Resurrection. The whole status of Peter as the rock upon which Jesus designated that his church be built would be a bit shaky if the masses knew the significance of the Risen Lord appearing to Mary, a mere woman, before Peter or any of the male disciples.

All of this time I was reading and studying, I continued to be involved in frequent meditations both individually and in small groups. During some of these meditations I had spontaneous regressions back to Palestine, for that is where I now recognized this place to be. In one of these, I found myself back in the marketplace wandering through the many stalls and looking at the wondrous variety of beautiful items offered for sale. I became aware that my hand was holding another's and I looked down to see a man's hand clasping mine. I felt warm and protected, safe and loved. He and I continued on in the marketplace. I pulled him with me from stall to stall laughing and exclaiming with the joy of sharing the market delights with him. I heard his deep, joyous laugh and knew that he enjoyed seeing the market through my eyes.

When the meditation ended and I finally opened my eyes, I was crying. Tears of joy and despair streamed down my face. The joy was that of being with him again, this man whom I loved more than life itself. The despair was in having to once again relinquish him and that glorious feeling of being so cherished and loved. I no longer had any doubt who this man was; this was Jeshua, the one the planet referred to as Jesus of Nazareth. I also knew my own identity in that time and place. Jeshua called me "Beloved"; others knew me as Mary Magdalene.

What a stretch it was, what a leap of faith to even entertain the idea that I, this insignificant woman living in the twentieth century, could have walked upon the earth with the most well known figure of the modern western world. How could I even consider that I could have loved and been loved in return by the man whom many revered as the Son of God? Talk about a colossal ego! Who did I think I was?

Still the memories kept coming and the flashes occurred even when I was not actively meditating. I saw us standing beneath an arbor, our hands ceremonially bound together with a cord or scarf, two engraved silver rings shining in the torchlight. I was aware of the presence of a small group of family and friends surrounding us and felt the love and acceptance from that group.

The most emotional regression occurred in a group situation. The facilitator began our journey into the past by suggesting that our Higher Self would lead us to the lifetime that most affects the current one. I recall asking within my heart that it not be Palestine again. I was beginning to doubt my ability to control the emotion that manifested with clear memories of that time. As I looked down at my feet, the next suggestion of the facilitator, I saw sandals and knew that I had returned again to that lifetime. Though I tried to resist, it was apparent that I needed to see more of that time. My soul led me to the place that I did not want to revisit, the place of the crucifixion.

I found myself crouched at the bottom of a rough wooden post that had been thrust into the ground. I placed my hands on the post and physically felt the rough wood and the splinters still present. My heart was filled with the deepest despair and I was weeping uncontrollably. I gazed in horror as warm blood dripped down on my hands from above. I could not look up to see the face of the man who had been so cruelly nailed to this wooden tool of execution. As I watched this scene from my past, the part of my mind still aware of the "me" in the present fought against allowing this overwhelming emotion to consume me and spill into the physical. My body tensed and when the regression ended, I reached for a floor pillow, held it close, and wrapped my arms around it trying to hold the emotion in check. Despite my need for control, I was quietly sobbing but was able to refrain from the hysterics that still threatened.

When I finally calmed down and was able to speak

without sobbing, I reassured the facilitator that I was fine and able to drive home unassisted. I cried all the way home remembering the feel of the wooden cross beneath my hands and the warmth of Jeshua's blood. There was no doubt that it was Jeshua nailed to the cross, no doubt that I witnessed his cruel execution, and no doubt that a part of me died with him that day. I knew there was more to see, more information I had to have to make the memories make sense.

Why remember them now? Why remember at all? That lifetime was 2000 years ago and those who shared that lifetime with me were not a part of my current life. Was there a reason I was recalling that time? What was I to do with the information I had already received? I was surely not prepared to call Oprah and share this with the world! I did not relish being publicly humiliated and stoned. The question was answered shortly thereafter.

On the evening of March 1, 1995, I facilitated the weekly Reiki healing session at the spiritual center where I spent much of my free time. I began with a guided meditation and then the small group of five took turns giving Reiki energy to one another. John stretched out on the massage table and each of the other four of us sat at his head, feet, and sides, placing our hands at the traditional Reiki healing points. The music was soft and gentle, reminiscent of angels singing and the subdued lighting in the sanctuary was conducive to our returning to a deep meditative state. It was in this state while giving Reiki that the next step in my remarkable journey occurred.

I was in deep meditation listening to the beautiful music. In my mind, my angel came to me and told me she had someone who wanted to speak with me. She "stepped" aside and I found myself face to face with the largest angel I could imagine. His wingspan was enormous and his face was close to mine. He introduced himself.

"I am Archangel Michael," he said, "and I would like to work with you. Please meet with me tomorrow morning at 7:00 with a pen and notebook to take down what I have to tell you."

"Yes, sir!" I answered. What else would you tell an Archangel, no?

The next morning I woke hearing Michael's voice. I looked at the clock. 6:45!

"Just a minute, Michael," I said. "You told me 7:00 on the dot. It's not quite seven and as a physical being, there are certain things I have to take care of when I first get out of bed before I can write in a notebook. Please wait until seven. I promise I will be ready to write your words then."

I took care of those physical things (like getting dressed, the bathroom, a glass of water, and daily medication) and sat at my dining room table at seven precisely with pen in hand. I said a prayer of protection and centered into a meditative state. Michael announced his presence and began speaking.

"I am Lord Michael," I heard and wrote his words.

I had to ask him to slow down a time or two but managed to capture all he told me.

His first message was to tell me that this would be an ongoing project to allow me to access information regarding the purpose of my mission on earth. He would also assist me in recalling the Palestine life and would fill in details as needed about important events. He would not be alone in this, he told me, and referred to other highly evolved spiritual beings that would be there, whether discerned or not, to help in this undertaking. The scope of the undertaking is something I am still discovering.

We agreed to meet everyday at seven for an hour of communication. I have three extra large college-ruled spiral notebooks filled with the writings I did with Michael and my other spiritual guides during the remainder of 1995 plus countless others filled with typed messages that have been written since then. I no longer write with them every day without fail as I did the first year due to time restraints, but know they are still with me guiding and protecting as before.

As I read others' books channeled by these same guides, I learned more about Lord Sananda, as he is called formally, and the spiritual hierarchy, the highly evolved spiritual beings who are of the Light and work only for the good of mankind and the glory of God/Creator/Universe. I discovered that he is the guardian of this part of the Universe and is most highly respected and loved among the spiritual hierarchy. I also found material that confirmed the feelings I had since childhood that what was being told to the masses as the truth of those years in Palestine was not the truth as seen and remembered by other souls who had shared in that very unique lifetime.

One morning, as I sat prepared to write, I felt the energy focus on my left side rather than the right, where Michael's energy usually manifested. I then heard a different voice.

"I am Lord Sananda," I wrote in surprise and then promptly dropped my pen.

Why I was so nervous at his presence I did not know, but nervous, honored, and shocked I was. His first words to me reassured me that his presence was due to his wish to assist me in remembering the Palestine life and transcribing those facts for future publication. Again, I dropped my pen.

Wait a minute, I thought. It took me how many months to accept that I might have been on the planet in the area of Palestine during the life of Christ. Then it took me several months more to accept that I might have known him. Then it took me months of deep introspection, prayer, and meditation to accept that I might have lived as Mary Magdalene. Now I was being asked to take a further step and announce this to the world! Did they think I was a fool? What kind of loony bird would write a story like this and risk being attacked by all the fundamentalist Christians in the world? Was I a masochist willing to be tarred and feathered, or worse, just to present this recollection of a remembered past life to a world that would reject it and me? Hah! I think not!

My curiosity about this life would not allow me to ignore it and the knowledge that I carried in a lot of karma and unfinished business from that life that needed to be resolved. So I continued writing and asking questions and meditating about that time and place.

Chapter 2

Channeling on March 9, 1995 with Archangel Michael

"Q: What can you tell me about Magdalene?

A: Magdalene was a definite handful. Her aged father spoiled her after the death of her mother and her pitiful cries for her mother softened the hearts of her siblings, so little real discipline was learned at an early age. She was rambunctious and free of spirit, loved life and delighted in the simple beauty of the countryside. She would rise early and greet the sunrise from the top of a nearby hill. Often she spent afternoons in quiet meditation in the garden where her mother was buried. There was a small arbor that supported grapevines and she sat beneath it in the shade contemplating life and wondering about her purpose in the scheme of things. As a young girl, her hair was often in wild disarray, for she loved to feel it blowing in the breeze. She loved Bethany, the gardens and hills of her father's estate, and truly did not have to learn the tasks of household management, for there were plenty of hired people to help with the upkeep of the estate and Martha was an excellent household manager.

She learned to read at an early age and spent many mornings and evenings in her father's library reading and discussing politics and the law. She kept her father company in his old age. Lazarus was too busy seeing to his father's business ventures and Martha with the running of the large household to spend much time in discussion. But Magdalene sat willingly with her father and learned much. He was a wise man with astute business skills and a keen mind for the law. All she learned of the world's geography and the political systems of the time she learned from him. Her knowledge protected and helped many of the group in later years. She was much more active in the new churches than any have suspected. She and Jeshua traveled extensively before the crucifixion, sometimes together, sometimes separately. Always then those who knew she was the Master's beloved wife accorded her much love and respect. Those who knew her only as Mary Magdalene respected her great knowledge and her underlying compassion for those in pain and sorrow. She did much to advance the teachings of Jeshua yet received no credit in history, but she wanted none. She was content to have the world ignore her presence by Jeshua's side. Her joy came from watching the faces of those who heard his words light up as the message of love and light was understood and accepted. Many times her heart overflowed with the joy and peace she experienced watching the face of Jeshua as he gently led the crowds to a new realization of God's love. Her children adored her. She was gentle and nurturing with them, lavishing her love and time on them when she was not traveling. Sarah, especially, voiced the determination to be just like her mother and at an early age developed a mature bearing that impressed and delighted Jeshua. Her sons were less attached to her but no less loving. They learned the law and their father's teachings at an early age and they, too, taught the Word to all who would listen.

Leaving Galilee was hard for the group, but it was necessary not only to preserve their lives, but also to spread the teachings. Magdalene spent many nights with Jeshua and others poring over maps while they planned in detail the pattern of teaching assignments. Think you that this was spontaneous and unrehearsed? This rivaled the best military strategy of the Roman Empire! Would that Alexander had had the benefit of Magdalene's keen mind. He could have conquered the whole planet, not just the civilizations that fell before him.

Q: Did Jeshua's parents approve of Magdalene and their relationship?

Some thought she was too aggressive at times and too public a figure to be wife to Jeshua. His mother did not approve of the marriage because of Magdalene's flighty ways as a young woman. In later years, she gave Magdalene the respect she earned and grew to love her as the mother of her grandchildren, if nothing else, but they were never close friends. Joseph was amused by Magdalene's "scandalous" behavior and rejoiced that his son had found in her a woman who enjoyed life and lived it to the fullest. He truly loved her and accepted her wholeheartedly. They had many long discussions by the fire late in the evening when Jeshua was traveling and the others in the household were asleep. The two had a deep and abiding friendship and Magdalene wept inconsolably at his passing to spirit."

* * * * *

This portrait matched the feeling of the first regression in which I was full of life and flirty. I got clear pictures of places and flashes of people and events as I re-read the writing. (I suppose I should mention that when I write with "the Guys", as I call them, I am channeling and have to re-read for content since I have little recall of what I am typing or writing after the fact.) So many details came to me that I had to write them down before they disappeared in a fog. As I made the list, I knew that I had to write what I was receiving.

Chapter 3

The three-year-old stood in the rain, her hand held tightly by her older sister as she watched the lifeless body of her mother lowered into the tomb that had been prepared for it. She felt so cold inside, so alone, even though Martha held tightly to her hand. She felt her brother's hand resting on her shoulder, but took no comfort in the warmth. She looked at her father resting against the giant stone that would seal them all forever from the woman who had nurtured and comforted the family. His head bowed in grief, the tears flowed freely for the love he had lost.

She tried to pull her hand from Martha's. Her father needed her now. But Martha's hold tightened.

"Magdalene, be still! The prayers are about to begin."

Ten-year-old Martha stood stoically, the rain dripping down her face, bitterly watching the ceremony. She had learned eagerly at her mother's knee the responsibilities of running the family's large household. The knowledge that she would have to do that very thing weighed like a stone in her stomach. She was too young to be mother to three year old Magdalene. Martha fought hard to overcome the fear and pushed down the grief that threatened to overwhelm her. He father would depend on her to come through for the family. She would not disappoint him.

Lazarus, too, felt the freedom of childhood slip away to be replaced with the burdens of responsibility. His father was devastated with the unexpected death of his wife and companion and could only sit in shock as the family made the arrangements. Thank God, Mary and Joseph had arrived from Nazareth in time to make arrangements for the burial and feeding the many friends and family members who had gathered. He knew Martha could not have coped with all the duties and responsibilities required.

He watched Joseph and the other men lower his mother into the tomb. He watched as Jeshua, Joseph's thirteen-year-old son, grabbed the shrouding cloth to help steady the body. Although the same age as Lazarus, Jeshua was slightly taller than he and seemed years older in bearing and wisdom. Close friends through childhood, he would miss Jeshua and his brother, James, dearly while they were gone. In just two days' time, they were scheduled to leave for Egypt to study with the learned priests at Heliopolis.

After the tomb was sealed, Martha burst into tears and was gathered into Mary's embrace. Joseph put one arm around Lazarus and the other around Simon, Lazarus' father, and led the two back to the house and shelter from the downpour. The rest of the mourners followed.

Magdalene ran to the stone that sealed the tomb and pounded her fist against it viciously, the tears streaming down her face.

"Mother, come back! Mother, come back! I need you. I'll be good, I promise! Please, Mother, please!"

Jeshua picked up the distraught girl and held her tight, cradling her until her sobs quieted into hiccoughs.

"I know you are sad, little one, but your mother did not leave you because you weren't a good girl. You know that, don't you?"

"Then why did she leave me? Doesn't she love me anymore?" Magdalene whimpered into Jeshua's shoulder.

"No, beloved one. She left because God, our Father, has need of her in heaven. Do you remember how she baked you honey cakes and made your father his very favorite lamb stew?"

Magdalene sniffed loudly and nodded.

"Well, God looked down from heaven and saw all the love that your mother had for her family and how special she made each of you feel. Then he looked around at all the children in heaven whose mothers are still here on earth and wondered if perhaps she would be willing to care for all those children just like she cared for you. God knew that

Martha would soon be old enough to take over the household. He also knew that if you knew about all those little children there who had no mother to love them or make them honey cakes that perhaps you would be willing to share your mother with all the souls and angels who live in heaven. Was he right, Magdalene? Can you be happy for your mother who now lives in heaven with the Father and his angels?"

Jeshua held her close and waited until her sobs were done. She wiped her eyes and nose with her sleeve and looked into his eyes.

"Do I have to be happy for me?"

Jeshua laughed softly and kissed the top of her head.

"No, sweet, you don't have to be happy for yourself. I know you are going to miss her very much. But you have Martha to tuck you in at night and Lazarus to play with you in the garden while your father tends to his business."

"Will you be here, too, Jeshua?"

"No, Magdalene. I have to go far away for a while to study, but I will come to see you as often as I can."

"Can I go with you? I promise I'll be good."

"No, Magdalene. I must go alone. But I promise I'll come back as soon as I can."

"Do you promise you'll come back? Will you wait for me to grow up? Then I can go with you. If you came back and married me, then I could go with you forever! Will you wait, Jeshua, please?"

Jeshua looked down at the little girl and smiling, gently wiped the tears from her cheeks.

"Yes, Magdalene. I'll wait for you."

"Do you promise? Cross your heart?"

"I promise. Cross my heart."

Jeshua carried her toward the house. Magdalene felt warm for the first time in days. She put her little arms around Jeshua's neck and held on tight. She knew, for the first time since her mother's death, that everything would be all right.

Chapter 4

Finally! I was out of the house and in the warmth of the sun where I longed to be. The warm breeze, one of the last of the summer, blew around me teasing long strands of my hair from beneath the tightly pinned veil that held it captive. If I had not been on my way to the marketplace, I would have yanked the pins out, tossed them into the bushes, and tied the veil around my waist to get it out of my way. But that would not be "seemly behavior" for a maiden of nineteen, as Martha again had reminded me just before my hurried escape. Nearly every day there was some kind of reminder of how a proper Jewish maiden should behave, especially one rapidly approaching official spinsterhood.

Spinsterhood! HA!! I kicked a stone in my path in sheer frustration. Spinster, indeed! Martha and Lazarus voiced the opinion that I should accept one of the many offers Father had received for my hand. What they did not know was that my heart had been promised long ago to the only man I would ever want to marry. When and if he ever returned to Galilee for good! Sixteen long years Jeshua and his brother, James, had traveled with their cousin John seeking wisdom and knowledge from every corner of the world. All I had to show for those long years of waiting were the three messages he had written to me and the brief visit to Alexandria.

The first message arrived on my thirteenth birthday as I left the world of childhood and became an adult. That first message had been written in China and found its way over the mountains and through the deserts by way of a spice caravan that stopped in Bethany on its way to Jerusalem.

"Beloved Magdalene," he had written, "I will be thinking of you as the lamp is lit at your birthday celebration. This day marks your entrance into womanhood. Let not the pretty words of your suitors turn your head, for I have not forgotten my promise to wait for you to grow up. Do you also remember? I will return when my studies are complete. Meanwhile, I hold your memory in my heart."

Pretty heady words for a thirteen-year-old girl, but they thrilled me still whenever I read them. I learned soon enough to keep secret Jeshua's messages to me. I shared the first one with Lazarus, who teased me unmercifully.

"Do you really think he is going to wait for a child to grow up before he marries? A rabbi is required by God to marry and have children. By the time you grow up, he will be too old!" Lazarus laughed and dismissed the thought from his mind.

"You did not see his face when he promised me," I thought. "I looked into his eyes and felt as though I was falling into a cyclone. I knew then, and I know now, that what he promised will come to pass."

My hand unconsciously found my heart and the locket that hid beneath my tunic. Just the feel of it brought a smile to my lips and warmth to my heart.

The locket and the second message arrived on my sixteenth birthday. My heart fluttered with excitement as I unwrapped the package that had traveled all the way from India in a shipment of exotic shawls and brilliantly colored silks. Jeshua had wrapped a beautiful peacock blue shawl around the locket and accompanying letter. The locket was silver with a Star of David engraved upon it and filigree worked around the edge.

The message filled my heart with joy.

"Beloved Magdalene. Keep this locket close to your heart and know that I think of you often. Remember my promise to you. I have not forgotten."

The memory of those words thrilled my heart and I smiled to myself as I touched the familiar outline of the locket that I kept hidden beneath my tunic. No one other than Martha and my father knew of its existence. My mind raced ahead to the third message from Jeshua received just three days previously.

"Beloved Magdalene," the message said. "I have completed my studies and will be returning to Galilee and my family. Think not that I have forgotten your presence in Bethany. Neither could I forget your presence in my heart. I cannot say what day I will return, but return to you I will."

Suddenly, a rush of love and joy filled me so strongly that I could no longer contain it. I pulled the tiresome veil from my hair, tied it about my waist and ran towards the marketplace, laughing at the birds that squawked their displeasure as they took to the sky in an effort to avoid my headlong flight.

I arrived at the marketplace disheveled and out of breath, my usual state of being. Josie called me to her fruit stand and offered me a ripe juicy fig. I accepted with thanks and helped myself to a dipper of water, most of which seemed to drizzle down my sleeve. I brushed the flyaway hair from my face and ate the fig with relish, all the while chattering to Josie about her family and mine and the preparation for Jeshua's return.

The juice from the fruit dripped down my chin and, unmindful of my appearance, I wiped my chin with my sleeve. Behind me I heard a low chuckle and a soft laugh. My heart leaped to my throat. I recognized his voice, his energy, even though I had not seen him in a year.

I whirled around and saw Jeshua, arms crossed, smiling indulgently. His smile turned to a grin and he opened his arms to me. With a shriek of joy, I flew at him. He picked me up and swung me around laughing until we were both dizzy. He lost his footing and we both tumbled headlong into the pile of rugs next to Josie's stand.

I laughed so hard I couldn't speak. As my laughter subsided, I became very aware of being in Jeshua's arms. We had both changed much the last year. He looked more peaceful and balanced and was by far, I noticed, the most handsome man I had ever seen. I had changed from an unawakened girl into a mature young woman. By the look in his eyes and the catch of his breath when our eyes met, he was as aware of the changes as was I.

A flash of memory of the previous year took me back to Alexandria where he had surprised me one afternoon and interrupted my studies in the Temple of Isis. I was thrilled to see him and a little shy of the way he studied me. He had matured in the years since we last saw one another, as had I. At least I hoped he would see me for the woman I had become and not the girl of ten that I had been. Then he smiled and opened his arms to me and I knew that he no longer saw me as a child.

We spent hours together that afternoon talking and getting to know one another. I told him of my studies with the Temple and my position as priestess. One of my duties would have normally been to dedicate men to the Mother Goddess in the rite of Sacred Marriage.

"Have you been asked to do this?" Jeshua asked.

"No," I answered. "The High Priestess, Alta, knows that I am promised to you and that I would never agree to give myself to another."

"I have come to Alexandria to seek dedication to the Goddess. I have studied and been initiated in many other religions and have sought God and his wisdom in each. I would now seek the wisdom of the Goddess. Would you be willing to share yourself with me for this purpose, the uniting of god and goddess? You may decline, Magdalene. I'm sure there is another who…"

"No, Jeshua. No other will do this. I will be honored to dedicate you. I must speak with Alta about the arrangements. How long will you stay in Alexandria?"

"I must leave with the morning tide."

I remembered little about that night's events. The wine had been laced with something to relax me so the spirit of the Goddess could more easily enter my consciousness, normally done when I was to speak the Goddess' words for those gathered. This would be different, though, and Alta explained the ritual to me, assuring me that the spirit of the Goddess would know how to proceed.

So that night, at sunset, Jeshua was led to the sacred chamber lit with candles and filled with flowers and the scent of incense. He found me standing beside the altar dressed in the sheer gown and flowered headdress of the Goddess. He reached for me and took my face in his hands.

"I come to the Goddess to ask for wisdom and to dedicate myself to truth." He kissed me gently. The energy of the Goddess filled me and I tingled from head to toe.

I woke to the bright light of morning shining through the window. I still lay in the sacred chamber. The flowers had wilted and the incense long burnt out. I was alone. The only evidence of the night's ritual was the spilled wineglass next to me and the slight smear of blood along my inner thigh.

Jeshua had sailed with the morning tide and I was left with only a faint memory of his presence.

Suddenly, a shadow fell on us, bringing me swiftly back to the present moment..

"Jeshua! You forget yourself!"

I looked up to see his mother standing there. She stared at me disapprovingly, her eyes as cold and hard as her voice had been. This was not the beautiful, loving Mary I remembered comforting Martha as our mother was buried. This haughty and imperious woman had the air of one who was used to having her every word obeyed without question.

Jeshua chuckled and helped me to my feet. I brushed the dust from my clothes and tried to make my hair more presentable. Mary's look of disapproval as she slowly looked me up and down made me very aware of my state of disarray and the dirt that clung to my face and hands still sticky from the fig. I felt the blood rushing to my face in embarrassment.

"I have to go," I stammered to Jeshua. "Will you come to supper tonight?"

Jeshua took my hand and looked deeply into my eyes.

"Yes," he said. "I would be honored."

I smiled and reluctantly let go of his hand. I mentally straightened my shoulders and faced Mary with the best smile I could muster.

"It was nice to see you again, Mary. Have a blessed afternoon."

As I turned to go, I heard her mutter "Harrumph!" under

her breath and Jeshua's admonishment, "Now, Mother..." I walked sedately until I turned the corner of the building and was out of sight. Then I ran all the way home as the implications of our meeting began to sink into my brain.

Jeshua was finally home! He had at long last come home to claim me for his own!

* * * * *

Our visitors arrived at dusk, Joseph, looking tired and noticeably older than the last time I had seen him, Mary Josephine, or Eena, as she was called, Jeshua's youngest sister, and James and Jeshua, looking as alike as if they had been twins. Yet I had no difficulty telling them apart. They had never been able to fool me, though they often tried during the years. Although alike in appearance, there was a gentleness about Jeshua that could not be disguised and a sparkle in his eye that I did not see in James, even though he was as full of life as Jeshua and shared his fondness for practical jokes.

I was so nervous through dinner that night I could scarcely swallow. Eena sat next to me and kept trying to distract me. She was nearing thirteen and I could see already the bloom of beauty and intelligence in her eyes. She, like me, was not content to sit idly by doing needlework or discussing the latest in fashion or neighborhood gossip. She could always be found at Joseph's knee, asking endless questions and trying to make sense of the universe.

When the meal was finished, Martha took Eena to the sitting room to show her the latest fabric from the East. My father, Joseph and James retired to my father's library and closed the door behind them in my face as I attempted to follow. Exasperated, I turned to Jeshua who was grinning broadly.

He held out a hand to me and without a word led me out to the garden. As we wandered through the garden in the bright moonlight, I pointed out the various flowering plants that my mother had planted, that I now so lovingly tended.

"This one was her favorite," I pointed out. "Can you

smell the fragrance? I think they are the loveliest I have ever seen." I stroked the petals of one of the blossoms I had picked. Jeshua took it gently from my hand and tucked it behind my ear. His hand caressed my cheek.

"Yes," he said softly, "they are lovely. But their beauty cannot begin to compare with yours."

"Come," he said, and led me to a secluded bench beneath a vine covered arbor. We sat silently for a moment watching the full moon rising over the crest of the hill and enjoying the peace and tranquility of the night. Soon, however, my curiosity got the better of me and I asked the first of the seeming hundred questions crowding my thoughts.

"Jeshua, are you home for good? Are your studies truly finished?"

He chuckled and held my hand in his. When he looked at me, I saw his regard for me as an equal and knew somehow that he would never treat my questions with anything other than respect.

"My studies with others have ended," he replied, "but the wise man never stops learning of God the Father and the many wonders of the universe that he has created."

"Tell me of the places you have been and the wonders you have seen!"

"I will tell you of one place in which I studied for some time with learned priests and accomplished Masters. It is in the land of Egypt where our people were held in bondage for so long, not so far from Alexandria, where the Temple of Isis stands. I was privileged to sit at the feet of those who are well versed in the ways of the heavens, who chart the movements of the very stars as they cross the skies from age to age. I even studied with Balthazar, he who charted the stars at my birth.. He was one of the sages who traveled to see the infant whose very birth would change the course of history. Or so he said. But I have no desire to be known in history. I exist only to serve the Father in Love and Light and to do His bidding."

"How do you know what the Father's will is for you? I

listen to the rabbis and Pharisees and I hear nothing that touches my heart, nothing that resonates with the love of the Father."

"Indeed, it is difficult to find the gentle love of the Father for his children in the harsh words written by the prophets. I think that perhaps one of the reasons I was chosen to learn from the wisest of teachers in the world, was so I may speak to all men, women and children of the great and bountiful love that God has for each and every one of us, just like the love of a parent for a child."

Jeshua's eyes darkened. The gleam of moonlight through the leaves illumined his face, but it seemed to me that the glow about him shone from within.

"There are many kinds of love, Magdalene," he said, gazing deeply into my eyes. "For years I have patiently waited for the right time and the right place to tell you of my love for you. You have lived in my heart for all my life, little one, ever since the day of your mother's burial when I promised to return for you. That was no idle reassurance to a child. I knew in my heart at that moment that there would be no other one for me. What of you, Magdalene? Is there another who has caught your eye? Or have you kept your heart for me?"

I smiled up at him and noticed with womanly pride that he wanted anxiously for my reply, as though he was uncertain of my answer.

"Another in my heart?" I asked. "How could there be room for another when you have haunted my every dream since my thirteenth birthday? Not one day has gone by that I have not wondered, 'What is Jeshua doing today?' Not a night has passed that I have not gazed at the stars wondering if those same stars shone down on you."

I touched my hand to his face feeling the softness of his beard. "Oh, Jeshua! How can you ask if there is another? There has been only you, could be only you, for you fill my heart completely. There is no room for any other love!"

He pulled me to him, setting me in his lap. He caught sight of the silver chain in the moonlight and tugged the locket gently from beneath my gown and held it in the palm of his hand.

"I wear it constantly and am never without it. Only Martha and my father even know I have it. I was afraid Lazarus would tease me as he did when your first letter arrived."

"You have always known that I would come back to you, haven't you, my sweet little one?"

"Yes, Jeshua. I have worn your locket close to me every day to remind me of your promise and of your presence in my heart. Those times when my courage faltered and my patience grew thin, especially each time I attended the marriage of a friend or cousin, I touched the locket, held it in my hand and felt the warmth of your love for me despite the distance between us."

Jeshua smiled and caressed my cheek.

"Now I have truly come back to you, beloved. Our fathers even now draw up the marriage agreement between our families. That is, of course, if this is what you truly desire."

At that moment I was filled with such intense joy and longing that I feared I would explode. I threw my arms about his neck and hugged him tight, the tears of joy trailing down my cheeks.

He pulled away to look into my eyes, and smiling gently, wiped my tears.

"And so, my little Magdalene, do you then consent to be my wife, now and for all time?"

"Oh, yes, Jeshua. Yes, my dearest love. Now and for all time!"

Then softly, gently, he held me closer and kissed me there in the garden, in the moonlight, beneath a thousand stars.

Chapter 5

The next six months were a whirlwind of activity. My father and Martha were determined that this would be the best wedding our family and friends had ever seen. Relatives I hadn't known existed had sent word of their desire to attend the wedding and friends of both families from as far away as Rome and Egypt sent word of their impending arrival. The home of Joseph and Mary, though quite comfortable, was not nearly large enough for the onslaught of the many visitors expected. Even our own estate in Bethany, large by any standards, was found to be lacking in needed space. In the end, Father rented a villa in Cana from a wealthy Hebrew landlord who was traveling extensively. He moved a delegation of servants and handymen in to complete the repairs and decorations that Martha and my future mother-in-law had decided upon. I stayed as far away from the preparations as I could. I only cared that Jeshua was to be my husband and I, his wife. All the rest was strictly show, as far as I was concerned.

I spent increasingly more time with my father in his study as he taught me the geography of the world, discussed the political machinery of the Roman Empire, the trade routes to the known corners of the world, and one or two that were known only to a select few tradesman like my father and Lazarus. I learned the difference between soft buttery leather and the improperly tanned sandals that disintegrated in the space of a month or two. I became adept at judging the strength of a fabric by noting the number of threads in the woof of the weave, and whether the gold design was woven into the threads of the scarf or merely painted on for show. As I learned some of my father□s business and the customs of trading, I began to sit in with my father's meetings with the caravan owners as they negotiated prices and terms of delivery. All this information would become invaluable to Jeshua and me in later days. Indeed, lives were saved many times due to knowing the inner workings of the trade world.

Jeshua was as busy as I was during the months leading up to the wedding ceremony. He and James spent much time in discussion with the more open minded of the rabbis in the area. Both were hailed as learned teachers and were often invited to speak at the synagogues. As word of their knowledge and wisdom spread, they began to travel separately. John ben Zebedee and one or more of his brothers often traveled with Jeshua and then with James as the invitations to speak grew in number. Occasionally Jude or Simon, Jeshua and James's brothers, traveled along.

As preparations for the wedding reached a fevered pitch, I began to see a side of Jeshua's mother that I had glimpsed only once, the day of Jeshua's return. There were times I heard her speaking rather sharply with Martha about certain arrangement for the feast. When I asked Martha about it, she only shrugged.

"I'm sure she only wants the best for you and Jeshua," she said. "After all, this is the oldest son, and Mary has mentioned that Jeshua's lineage goes back to King David. Wouldn't it be exciting if Jeshua were actually the legitimate heir to the Throne of Israel?"

My heart grew cold at Martha's words. Exciting? No. Dangerous, deadly, frightening, those were the descriptions that tore at my mind. My father had trained me too well in the political intrigues of the Romans and their puppet king, Herod. If treachery was personified, it would surely manifest in the body of Herod, who would stoop to any act of deceit to keep the throne of his father, bought with the gold of his people and kept by the brute force of Rome's presence in Galilee.

No, my heart did not care for the idea of Jeshua's being the rightful heir or the possibility that this bit of information might one day find its way to Herod's ear. Just the thought of Herod's attention focusing on Jeshua, or any of us, gave me a shiver of real fear.

It's funny how time plays tricks with one's mind. I was so anxious to be Jeshua's wife, to preside over his home, bear his children, grow old with him, even the thought of quiet evenings alone in front of the fire filled me with joy. The months seemed to drag so slowly through the fall and winter. I thought spring would never appear in our little corner of the world.

Then suddenly, overnight it seemed, the time came to move our families and the entourage of servants and hired help needed for the week long festivities to the seaside villa at Cana. The estate was huge. Jeshua□s family stayed in one remote wing while I stayed with my small family in another. The bridal suite that had been prepared for us was on the upper floor toward the rear of the house, removed far enough from the rest of the rooms to afford Jeshua and me the real privacy we desired.

Three days before the wedding, the quests began to arrive. In no time at all it was very clear that we had grossly underestimated the number of people who would attend. The huge house was filled to overflowing with people, children, and servants. Tents were pitched on the grounds and a huge outdoor kitchen and dining area set up. Most of the growing crowds were fed there, keeping the indoor dining areas for immediate family and close friends.

Jeshua and I managed to steal a few moments alone together during the last few hours before our wedding day. I was growing more nervous with every moment. I never doubted that he and I were meant by God to be together, nor did I doubt the depth of his immense love for me. On the contrary, I was beginning to doubt my ability to be a proper wife to Jeshua. It was his mother who planted the seed of doubt in my mind.

I never imagined that Mary loved me as a daughter, but I hoped that someday she would come to at least have a fondness for me because I was Jeshua's wife, if for no other reason. The evening before the wedding, I had trouble sleeping and went out onto the balcony beside my room. In the garden beneath, I heard Mary speaking with Joseph. It certainly had not been my intention to eavesdrop, but Mary's voice was hard and cold and was carried up to me on the evening breeze.

"I find it hard to believe that you actually consented to Jeshua's request for a marriage contract with that girl. In all the years we have known Simon's family I don't think I have ever seen her in a presentable state. Her hair is in a constant state of disarray and she knows nothing about running a household. How in the world can Jeshua be expected to hold his head up in the community with a wife who cannot even prepare the simplest dish or keep order in his home? Heaven knows what will happen when they have children! I tell you, Joseph, Jeshua may well rue the day he ever married that wild girl!"

"Mary! Keep your voice down! I do not want you upsetting Simon or more importantly, Magdalene. I will not have her come to the wedding arbor with your hateful words upon her heart. You would feel the same of any woman Jeshua loved, but you feel even more strongly about Magdalene because she refuses to be intimidated by you. Leave her alone, Mary. For Jeshua's sake, do not let your heart be closed to her." Joseph's voice was clear and strong as he tried to reason with her.

"Mark me well, Joseph, this girl will be trouble."

"Enough, Mary. Go to bed. We have a long day ahead of us."

Mary entered the house. Joseph looked up at the balcony, almost as though he knew I was standing there. I stood there, arms wrapped around myself. I was in shock at what I had heard. I had never tried to deceive myself into thinking that she had any affection for me, but I was totally unprepared for the virulence I heard in her voice.

I stood there, feeling the darkness of spirit all around me. I knew Mary was very close to Jeshua. As her first born son, he had always been her favorite. Had she shared with him her views, the opinion that I would not be a good wife to him? For the first time since Jeshua had told me he would return for me when I was three, I began to have doubts about my ability to be the kind of wife that Jeshua deserved.

"Magdalene." Joseph's voice beside me startled me into awareness. He had climbed the stairs to the balcony when he saw my stricken look.

"Magdalene, you cannot allow her words to affect you or to begin to doubt yourself. You are Jeshua's love and the only one with whom he could be happy. Mary says these things because she does not understand your exuberance for life and does not approve of the freedom of spirit you exhibit. Those are the very things about you that Jeshua delights in. There will always be someone available to run the household and see to all the details that would drive you mad with boredom."

Joseph placed his hands on my shoulders and turned me to face him.

"My dear, there is only one woman in all the world that makes Jeshua's eyes light up, only one woman that causes his heart to race, only one woman who can support him in the work of God that he is here to do. That woman is you, Magdalene, only you."

He pulled me to him and enveloped me in a fatherly hug. I promptly burst into tears.

"I, for one, am delighted that my son has chosen you for his wife. This family can use the addition of someone who loves fun and has a love for life. Mary tends to keep tight reins on everyone. I think you'll be good for all of us, especially Jeshua."

My sobs subsided and I became aware not only of the warmth of Joseph's embrace, but of a strange tingling sensation. I opened my eyes and saw a faint blue glow surrounding us. I gasped and pulled back, but Joseph held me a moment longer until the tingling ceased and the glow faded.

"You actually felt that?" he asked.

I nodded. "What happened? What was that tingle, and the blue light! I've never seen anything like it!"

"And you saw too. Magdalene, you obviously have gifts

that you are unaware you have. When you and Jeshua have recovered from the rigors of the wedding, speak to him of this. He will be able to show you many wonderful things."

"Did you do that?"

Joseph smiled at me.

"It's a gift from the Father, my child, a way to balance the emotions. It's nothing to be frightened about."

"Oh, I'm not frightened! I thought it was wonderful. Can Jeshua do this, too?"

"You'll have to ask him yourself. Now. The hour is late. To bed with you. We can't have the bride show up with shadows under her eyes."

Joseph kissed my cheek, turned, and started down the stairs. He stopped, looked back over his shoulder, and chuckled.

"There seems to be someone waiting in the garden hoping to have a word with you. He's there in the shadows of the arbor."

I watched Joseph descend the staircase. Jeshua stepped out from the shadows and embraced his father. Then he looked up at me and opened his arms. I ran down the steps into his arms and felt, not for the first time, as though I had been welcomed home. He held me close for a moment and then pulled me into the shadows of the arbor for a kiss. When our lips parted, my heart felt deprived of the very warmth of existence.

"Only a few more hours, my love," he whispered into my hair, "and we will never be parted again." He nibbled playfully at my ear sending delightful shivers up and down my spine. I snuggled closer, but the overheard conversation preyed heavy on my mind.

"Jeshua," I said tentatively, "may I ask you something?"

"My love, you can ask me anything."

"Do you... do you think I'll be a good wife to you?"

Jeshua threw back his head and laughed.

I pinched his arm and waited until his laughter had quieted.

"I'm serious, Jeshua. I never realized that perhaps I

might not be the best wife for you. I know very little about running a household, or cooking, or sewing..."

"Magdalene! Do you truly think I want to marry you in order to have a woman to clean my house?"

He held my face between his two hands and looked into my eyes.

"I have traveled the world for many years, visited the wonders of the world, learned marvelous mysteries, and seen the most beautiful women of every land and race. But you, my darling funny girl, with your hair blowing in the breeze, are the only woman that has haunted my every dream, filled my every thought and brought joy and happiness to my heart. We'll hire someone to run the house, but you are the only one with whom I could ever share my life. Magdalene, I love you more than life itself."

He wiped the tears from my cheek with his thumb and gently kissed me. I threw my arms around his neck and clung to him for a long moment, relieved that Mary's words did not reflect Jeshua's feelings.

Suddenly we heard footsteps approaching and Martha's voice called to me.

"Magdalene? Come to bed! It is near the midnight hour and you are not supposed to see each other until the wedding! Come along!"

I kissed Jeshua one more time and smiled.

"The next time we kiss, I will be your wife!"

"Finally!" Jeshua replied.

Martha took hold of me and pulled me back to the house. I heard Jeshua's soft laugh. The sound of it warmed my heart through the long hours of the night until the sun rose bright and glorious on my wedding day.

Chapter 6

Mid afternoon found me pacing like a caged animal in my room. Martha had kept me confined all day so as not to see Jeshua, or he me, until the greeting of the bridegroom. Had he not been staying on the same estate, I would have had the run of the house until time to dress for the ceremony, but because of his presence, I was forced to stay in my room all day. As the sun began its descent toward the horizon and the hour grew closer to the time of our joining, I grew more and more nervous. Bethel called it wedding jitters.

"The same thing happened to me when Lazarus and I got married," she said, trying to reassure me. "The marriage was arranged between my father and yours and we really didn't know each other very well. I tell you, when I thought of becoming a wife to a man I barely knew, I nearly panicked. By the time he and the others of the bridegroom's party arrived, I was so nervous, I would have called it off if I could have."

She smiled wistfully and lovingly patted her belly, large with her third child.

"I'm certainly glad I married him, Magdalene. Lazarus is a wonderful husband and father. God has blessed us greatly."

"Were you really this nervous?" I asked.

"I'm not sure nervous is the right word for what you are feeling. Part of you is restless being cooped up indoors. Part of you is probably a little anxious about this whole big show of a wedding." She grinned broadly.

"But I'll bet the biggest part of you is anxious to have Jeshua all to yourself."

I could feel the blood rush to my face and covered my cheeks with my hands, but I wasn't quick enough to hide my grin from Bethel.

"I knew it!" she said, and we both laughed.

An hour before sunset, Martha and Bethel accompanied by Eena and Mary Elizabeth, another of Jeshua's sisters, came to help me dress for the ceremony. Martha fussed with my dress and hair, adjusting endlessly the layers of fine translucent Egyptian linen. Bethel brushed my hair until it shone, pulled the top and sides back, and braided white ribbons into it, letting the bulk of it hang down my back. Eena handed me a pendant, a silver circle on which had been fixed a raised six pointed star.

"James sent this to you,□ she said. "He told me that there is a special significance to this that Jeshua will explain to you. He said you would discover again one of the great mysteries of the world."

"Thank you, Eena," I replied. I hugged her tight and then she helped me put on the pendant, being careful not to disturb my hair.

I stood before the looking glass that my father had shipped from Rome and tried to see myself the way Jeshua would shortly see me. Would he see the love shining forth in my eyes or would he notice the nervousness, my trembling hands? Would he see the woman within that longed to be freed from the confines of convention, whose spirit longed to soar about the clouds? Or would he see the young nineteen-year-old who trembled on the brink of life with the only man she had ever desired, uncertain of the future, knowing of his greatness and wondering where she would fit into his world?

I gazed at my reflection. The image before me seemed to shift in three, the child I had been, the young woman I was at present, innocent of the ways of the world, surrounded by the solid core of her family and secure in their love.

But there in the background I could see the Magdalene of the future. She was older, wiser. She looked as though she had borne the weight of the world on her shoulders and come through stronger, triumphant. She looked back at me with such compassion, such sorrow, as though she knew full well what lay ahead, what fears I would face, what challenges I would have to overcome. Yet, I drew strength from the vision of this woman of the future, the me that I could become. This vision gave me a glimpse of the future, a glimpse that gave me the sure knowledge that no matter what lay ahead, I would rise to the challenge and triumph.

"Magdalene, look! Here they come!" Mary Elizabeth's voice cut into my reverie.

I joined her at the window and saw the bridegroom's party bright with torches and lamps, the light picking up the rich colors of their clothing and in some cases the flushed faces of the bridegroom's friends and brothers. It looked as though some had begun tasting the wine earlier in the day. I strained to see Jeshua emerge from the guesthouse to which he and the other unmarried men had been relegated days earlier by Martha. He and James stepped out of the doorway at the same moment. They were so alike, though Jeshua was the elder, that only by their clothing could one tell them apart.

They stepped into the center of the bridegroom's party. As the young men formed a procession around them, Jeshua looked up to my window. Although darkness had settled, I knew his eyes sought mine. I felt his love reach out to me, felt the warmth of his love touch my heart and wrap around my soul driving away all doubts, all fears, all misgivings.

The door opened and my father entered. The others left us alone and prepared to join the bride's procession to greet the bridegroom. My father embraced me for a long moment and when at last he held me at arms' length to look me over, I noticed the tears in his eyes.

"My dearest Magdalene," he said, "I am greatly blessed by God that He has allowed me to live long enough to deliver you into Jeshua's hands for safekeeping. I have lived only to see this night, to see you become the bride of he who brings into this world the Light and Love of the Father. I will miss you, though, my dear. My library will seem empty without you."

"But Father," I said smiling, "you know we are to live with you until our own house is ready. You will not have to miss me at all for quite some time."

There was a knock and Lazarus opened the door.

"They are at the gate, Father. It's time to greet the bridegroom."

I turned and picked up the gauzy veil that Martha had draped on the bed. I handed it to my father who draped it carefully over my hair. He kissed me gently before covering my face and carefully led me out of my room and down the stairs to meet the man with whom I would share the rest of my life.

The ceremony was held outside due to the number of guests. The immediate family members had already taken their place beneath the arbor that would serve as the wedding canopy. The arbor and surrounding yards were ablaze with the light of dozens of torches and lamps. The bridegroom's party made a path for Jeshua and James. My attendants did the same for my father and me. And so, Jeshua made his way to the arbor from the guesthouse as my father and I arrived at the door to the house.

Jeshua watched as we made our way through the guests to join him beneath the arbor. My father embraced me and placed my hand in Jeshua's then took his place beside Lazarus and Martha who stood on my right. Mary, Joseph and James stood to the left of Jeshua with the other brothers and sisters close behind.

The High Priest began the ceremony. My father had been able to persuade Caiphas to preside over the ceremony by appealing to his political ambition. To be seen by so many people in high places who had real influence and clout was too good an opportunity to be missed. Caiphas was accompanied by an entourage that included Joseph of Arimathea, one of Jeshua's uncles and an old friend of both families.

Caiphus' voice droned on, but I heard not a word. I had eyes only for Jeshua. I was aware only of the warmth of my hand in his and the burning look in his eyes as they sought mine beneath the almost sheer veil. I made the appropriate responses and listened as Jeshua did the same. Finally, he raised the bottom of my veil to allow me to sip the wine from the wedding chalice. The wine warmed me all the way down. Jeshua handed the chalice back to the High Priest and then he turned to me and lifted the veil from my face, folding it over my hair. He gazed into my eyes as the last blessing was pronounced, then kissed me softly on each check.

The onlookers burst into shouts of joy and applause and the musicians began a joyous song. We were rushed by family and friends eager to embrace the newly wed couple and soon we were separated. I saw Jeshua's head briefly above the crowd before he was again hidden by the exuberant throng of well-wishers. It seemed the hugs and good wishes would never end. My head began to swim with the lack of food and the closeness of the crowd, and I clasped Martha's arm for support.

"What is it, Magdalene? You're so pale," she said.

"Make way for the bride!" she called. "Bethel, bring food and wine for Magdalene. Where is Jeshua? They should be seated at the table by now."

Within moments, Jeshua reached my side and we were seated at the table. Bethel brought a plate heaped with tempting morsels and Lazarus appeared with two cups of wine.

"Jeshua, see if you can get her to eat. She's not had a bite of food all day. No wonder she nearly fainted!" Bethel instructed Jeshua softly, so as not to give rise to undue rumors of my health.

Jeshua nodded his thanks and turned a semi-stern look to me.

"You haven't eaten? For heaven's sake, why not? Surely they gave you at least bread and water in your prison room today!"

He took my hand when I laughed at his remark and kissed my open palm.

"I hope you are not frightened of me, Beloved. I would never hurt you, nor would I allow any other to do so."

"No, Jeshua, not frightened. A little nervous, perhaps. I could not eat earlier. Every bit I took seemed to stick in my throat."

"Then let us try now, my little Magdalene."

He plucked a grape from the mound of food before us and put it to my lips.

"Here, Beloved. Taste the sweetness of the grape. It is not nearly as sweet as your lips."

I blushed and took the grape thinking that he would busy himself at his own plate so I could slow the rapid beating of my heart and collect my thoughts. He was determined to see my plate empty, however, and continued feeding me with his own hand, alternating phrases of love with nonsensical urgings as one would use to a small child. I blushed at the phrases of love and giggled at his silliness.

"Come, little Magdalene, just one more taste of fig. Did you know that eating figs will make your hair curly? Come, sweetness, just one more little bite."

"Jeshua, please! Enough!" I begged laughing. "I am so full now that I may have to loosen my clothing!"

"Ah, Magdalene," he whispered, leaning closer, "That is something better done in private. I am looking forward to assisting you in that very task."

Jeshua took my hand and made lazy circles in the palm of it with his thumb, all the while gazing into my eyes. I looked into his clear blue eyes and felt the love, saw the desire for me, and knew again that there could never be another that would so touch my heart and soul.

Hours later, it seemed, Martha and Bethel came to take me to our bridal chamber. The other unwed girls of my party stood on the stairs lighting my way. The room was ablaze with candles and fragrant with the masses of spring flowers that were arranged in bowls and vases. A tray of fruit, cheese and bread had been prepared and a large carafe of wine with two goblets waited on the bedside table.

They stripped me of my wedding finery and dressed me in a sheer linen gown of Grecian design. Bethel removed the ribbons from my hair, brushed it till it glimmered in the candlelight, and retied it with a ribbon at the nape of my neck. I took my place in the huge bed and sat against the back of it, pulling the covers up to my neck.

We could hear the raucous laughter of the men in the hall as they escorted Jeshua to the room. Martha opened the door at his knock and looked over at me with tears in her eyes.

"Be good to her, Jeshua. She has known only love and kindness," she said.

Jeshua embraced her quickly.

"And she shall know none other from me, my sister dear. Do not be concerned. She is dearer to me than life itself."

The party of men started to enter the room, but Jeshua blocked their way.

"We appreciate you all being with us to celebrate our union tonight and we thank you for the generous outpouring of your love and good wishes for us. But Magdalene is weary and I feel I can attend to her needs without help."

The friends and family burst into laughter and rowdy comments.

"James, Lazarus, perhaps you can direct our friends and companions to the vat of new wine that the steward has just opened. I am told it was the best of last year's harvest."

I heard James' voice in the hall.

"Jeshua is right, my friends. The wine is excellent, the music superb, and wait until you see the dancing girls from Nubia sent by our friend, the Emir..."

The women giggled at Jeshua's impatient gesture and followed the men down the stairs and out to the feast that continued without our presence. Jeshua shut the door and barred it to keep misdirected guests from entering.

He looked around the room at the many candles and then to me. I sat very still with the covers pulled up to my chin watching Jeshua's movements. I was well versed in the ways of a man and a woman having spoken at length with Bethel and I received her candid advice along with the stories of her experience. Daydreaming about loving Jeshua as my husband was one thing. Having this as an imminent event was something else entirely.

I trusted Jeshua implicitly. I knew that never would he willingly cause me anxiety or pain. Yet I could not control the fear that began to build within.

He must have known what I was feeling, for he looked again at the blazing lights and said softly, "I do not think we need all this light, do you?"

I shook my head.

One by one, he blew out all the candles save the one beside the wine carafe. He never took his eyes off me as he moved about the room blowing out the candles. He came to the side of the bed and made a show of stretching and yawning. Then he sat on the bed and undid his sandals. He stood again and looked at me with such love and desire, then blew out the remaining candle and the room was plunged into darkness. I heard the rustle of his clothing as he removed it and let the garments fall to the floor. The bed gave with his weight and then I felt the warmth of his shoulder next to me, felt his breath on my hair.

"Are you cold, Magdalene? You are trembling. Come. Lie in my arms, dearest. Let me warm you."

He put his arm around me, pulled me close, and then moved us down to lie together, my head on his shoulder. His arms held me firmly but gently to him. I tentatively rested my hand on his chest and giggled as the soft curls tickled my hand.

Jeshua brushed a trail of soft kisses across my forehead and down my cheek. He kissed the corners of my mouth and then placed his lips on mine. All the fear, all the nervousness was forgotten in that moment as the love we had carried for each other all those long years was ignited and flamed into passion hot and bright.

Suddenly I was heat from my toes to my face. We slowly uncovered the mysteries of one another, the secrets that our bodies had shared with no other. As the moments of completion neared and he finally claimed me for his own, I knew that God had placed me here in this time and this place to share my life with this gentle man, this noble soul. The love we shared exploded into a thousand blue white stars and

I cried out his name as he called out mine.

* * * * *

Late in the night I woke shivering. I was alone in the room. I pulled the covers up wondering why Jeshua was gone. Suddenly the door opened slightly and in he slipped with a lighted candle. He smiled when he saw I was awake.

"I went looking for a sharp knife," he said, showing me a small knife in his hand. "Where is your locket?"

"I think it's over there, somewhere," I said, pointing to the pile of bedding at the foot of the bed that had been hastily pushed aside.

Jeshua rummaged through the pile and gave an "Aha!", holding up the locket triumphantly. He removed his robe and climbed into bed next to me.

"May I have a lock of your hair?" he asked.

"Of course, Jeshua, but why?"

"I'll show you in a moment." He carefully chose a long strand of my hair from underneath so it would not show and cut it off. He then did the same with his own. I watched as he wove the strands of hair, his dark and shiny, mine dark auburn with a slight curl, together into a circular braid. When he was finished, he pushed a hidden clasp on the locket causing it to spring open. He placed the braid of our hair in the hidden recess of the locket and closed it, then placed the chain around my neck so the locket rested over my heart. He took my face in his hands and looked intently into my eyes.

"We are now joined for all time," he said, "body to body, heart to heart, soul to soul. Nothing can ever come between us, in this world or any other. Wherever I am, there are you in my heart. Wherever you are, there am I in your soul. From the creation of this world until the end of the ages, we are destined to be as one. From now throughout all eternity, you are the only heart I will love, yours the only body I desire, your love the only love I crave."

He kissed me gently and wiped the tears that fell unnoticed down my cheek. He touched the locket gently.

"The braid of our hair within this locket is a physical

symbol of our love, our union on all levels. We are now one, Beloved, in the eyes of man and in the eyes of the Father, who made us both. I have loved you all your life, my darling Magdalene, and I thank God that finally I can hold you, caress you, and show you how very much you mean to me."

"Oh, Jeshua," was all I could say before he pulled me to him again.

"This must be heaven," I thought, "oh, God, do not ever let this end between us."

* * * * *

I was given information about the locket in a channeling done with Jeshua after this was written.

"The woven hair in the locket was indeed a true memory, my Beloved. The tenderness of that moment on our wedding night lives in me still. You wore that locket every day of our life together. You relinquished it only in death. Our daughter kept it and passed it on to our granddaughter. It was a treasured family heirloom for hundreds of years; it may still exist somewhere."

Chapter 7

The wedding feast continued another six days. We stayed isolated in our bridal chamber for two days savoring the privacy and the leisurely discovery of one another, rejoicing at the long awaited celebration of our love. On the third day, we reluctantly dressed and made our way down to the revelry that still continued. We were greeted and teased by all. Jeshua saw my blush and kept me within the protection of his embrace, scowling at those who crossed the boundary of good taste with their remarks. We sat with our closest friends laughing and joking and partaking of the excellent food that was set before us.

Late in the afternoon, the steward approached Mary as she sat with her group of friends and admirers and informed her that the wine supply was running low. She waved him off and then approached our group.

"Jeshua, may I speak with you?" she asked.

"Of course, Mother," he replied, and walked apart with her for a moment.

"Jeshua," I heard her say, "We are running out of wine. We have had so many more guests than expected. You have mastered many things, my son, many wonderful things. Can you not assist in this situation? We cannot run out of wine! It is unthinkable!"

Jeshua patted her arm consolingly.

"Mother, I understand your concern. None of us wants to disappoint our guests. But it is not yet time for me to reveal the true nature of who I am to the world. Be at peace about this. Trust in God's good bounty."

"But, Jeshua..." she protested.

"Mother, please. All will be provided." He kissed the top of her head and smiled, then returned to my side.

Mary went to the wine steward and instructed him to obey the words of her son, gesturing to the group, which included James, Jude, and us. The steward nodded at her, then shrugged his shoulders to his companion and sat on the low stone wall next to the gate to await further orders.

The afternoon was warm with a pleasant breeze. We laughed and talked with our friends enjoying good company and good food. At one point, Jeshua motioned for the server to refill our goblets with wine.

The wine left in the pitcher refilled only one goblet.

"I'm so sorry, sir," the server stammered." This was the last of the wine. Your mother ordered more wine from the merchant, but it cannot be delivered until tomorrow."

"No more wine, brother? This is serious, indeed!" James stood and clapped his hand on Jeshua's shoulder. "You must see to this. Never let it be said that the wedding feast of Jeshua and Magdalene lacked for a thing."

Jeshua went to the wine steward and motioned to several large vats of water. He and the steward inspected them. Jeshua asked the steward to have servers come forward with pitchers in which to pour the contents of the large jars.

"Watch him, Magdalene. See what happens," James whispered.

Jeshua extended his hand over the large jars of water, closed his eyes briefly, and appeared to be praying. He then opened his eyes and grinned at James.

"What happened, James? What did Jeshua do?"

"Just wait and see, Magdalene."

The wine steward came hurrying to Jeshua's side with five or six servers, each carrying a large wine pitcher. He motioned for the steward to tip the first jar and poor the contents into a pitcher. The steward hesitated for a moment, then tipped the jar. Out poured, not water, but wine! The server was so surprised, he dropped the pitcher to the ground, spilling the wine and smashing the pitcher. The others quickly filled their pitchers and began serving the guests.

James motioned for more wine and held both our cups to

be filled. The fragrance of the wine as it poured into my glass filled the air with its sweetness. James held his cup close and inhaled the fragrance. Then he took a sip and held it in his mouth savoring the taste before swallowing. He looked up at Jeshua, who had returned to his chair, and grinned broadly.

"An excellent contribution to the festivities, Jeshua. I applaud you."

"It meets with your approval, then?" Jeshua asked.

"You know it does, Jeshua. This batch is even better than before. You must have been practicing."

James and Jeshua laughed together, then we all sampled more wine. It was by far the best wine I had ever had, and that, considering the amount of wine from far away places that my father had access to, was saying a lot. No one at our table seemed to be at all surprised that Jeshua had just turned six huge jars of drinking water into the finest of wines merely by holding his hands over the jars and praying softly. Finally, my curiosity got the better of me and I moved closer to Jeshua.

"May I ask you a question, Jeshua?" I whispered.

"Of course, Magdalene. You may ask me anything."

"How did you do that? Is this something you learned while studying with the Masters?"

"Yes, this and more. The ability to change the physical properties of one thing to another is not something easily done, nor is it something done for amusement. The ability is a gift from the Father and should be used only for the good of others. This very excellent wine is a gift from God, the Father, who made us all. It is a blessing for our marriage, Magdalene."

Jeshua reached for me and pulled me to him, sitting me firmly in his lap. The warmth of the afternoon sun and the wine coupled with the company of good friends made us relaxed and mellow. I began feeding Jeshua bits of honey cake, grapes, and bread. We drank liberally of the excellent wine and laughed most of the afternoon away.

James regaled the group with stories of Jeshua as a

child, remembering with glee all the embarrassing details. I laughed so hard I nearly fell off Jeshua's lap. As a lark, I took his cup of wine and held it behind my back so he couldn't see it. He looked around me to the table then looked on the ground on each side of the chair. Still he could not find his cup of wine. Jude and John ben Zebedee leaned against each other giggling helplessly at the sight of Jeshua searching for his wine. Even James, usually the staid and somber brother, was grinning from ear to ear and shaking his head in amazement.

"Magdalene!" Jeshua said firmly.

"Yes, Jeshua?"

"Magdalene, what happened to my wine? Have you seen my cup? I know it was here a moment ago!"

I tried hard to keep a straight face, not very easy to do when all the others were laughing uproariously at Jeshua's expression.

"Why, no, Jeshua. I do not know what happened to your wine. Did you finish it perhaps, and send the cup off with the server?"

"No, I'm sure I didn't. It was right there a moment ago, right next to yours. Are you sure you haven't seen it?"

I put on the face of the dutiful wife and replied, "No, Jeshua. I haven't seen it."

Jude and John dissolved into fits of laughter and James hid his face in his arms on the table, his sides shaking with uncontrollable laughter.

Jeshua's arm suddenly wrapped around me and his hand grasped the cup I had been hiding.

"What is this, woman? Are you trying to keep my wine from me?" He looked so stern that I burst into laughter and rumpled his hair. He did not even smile. My heart dropped. Apparently, my teasing had gone too far.

"Jeshua, I'm sorry," I stammered quickly. "It was done in jest."

"Jest!" he shouted. "You make fun of me in front of our guests and call it jest?"

I jumped from his lap in sudden fright and watched as he

stood to glare down at me.

"Woman," he said sternly, "I am your husband. I will have respect!"

With that he picked me up and threw me over his shoulder.

"Friends, I fear 'tis time to teach this unruly wife of mine some manners. I beg you to excuse us." He grabbed a pitcher of wine from the incredulous server and stormed toward the house. The crowd of onlookers was silent for a moment, then again burst into laughter that was louder than before.

I pounded uselessly with my fists against his back. How dare he treat me like this!

"Jeshua! Put me down this instant! How dare you treat me like this! Jeshua! Jeshua!"

Suddenly his hand slapped my backside, not hard, not painfully. But the fact that he raised his hand at all to me struck real fear in my heart.

"Woman, be still, or it will go the worse for you!"

Oh, Father in Heaven! I thought. Surely Jeshua was not a man to beat his wife! Surely, I could not have misjudged him so badly. Could I?

When we reached our chamber, he slammed the door behind us and barred it. He let me slip from his grasp and turned his attention to the wine, pouring us each a cup. He turned to me with a cup in each hand and found me cowering in the corner, my eyes wide with fear and my trembling arms crossed in front of me in defense.

Instantly, he was contrite.

"Magdalene, sweetheart, no! Please do not tell me you thought I was serious, that you think I could ever raise my hand to you, of all people! Magdalene. Beloved!"

He opened his arms to me and after a hesitant moment, I ran to them with a sob. He held me to him for the longest, letting me cry out all the fear, all the imagined hurt. Then he led me to the bed and cuddled me on his lap, reassuring me with his tender words and soft caresses, showing me in every possible way of the love he had for me.

"Jeshua," I said much later, "why did you carry me away

like that?"

"Magdalene, my love. I could not stand one more moment of having you so near and not being able to touch you. I had to bodily carry you into the house or risk a scandal by kissing you senseless right out in the open in front of our guests."

"What about James and John and the rest? Whatever must they think?"

"They won't be concerned. I grinned at them and winked as I reached for the wine. They know you weren't in danger of being beaten."

"So that's why they were laughing!"

I jumped from the bed and stormed to the door.

"Wait till I get my hands on them!"

Jeshua reached me and pulled me away from the door just as I was reaching for the bar.

"There is only one place for you dressed the way you are at this moment," he said. "And that is not downstairs!"

He swept me off my feet, deposited me right in the center of our bed, and proceeded to kiss me senseless.

* * * * *

After the evening meal, we wandered around the estate greeting friends and family who had come to share in our happiness. About half the guests had departed, but some of them lingered on enjoying the warm evening breeze that blew softly and the music of the evening's entertainment. We saw James and John seated on the ground watching a group of Nubian dancers. We hurried to join them, watching the graceful movements of the dancers.

I glanced at Jeshua's face as he watched with interest, perhaps too much interest for my thinking. A stab of jealousy ran through me. Did he think me as pretty as them? Did he find them more desirable than he did me?

As though hearing my thoughts, John leaned over and whispered to me.

"They are leaving tomorrow, you know. I'd wager that you could persuade one of them to teach you that dance, perhaps even sell you a costume. Jeshua seems to be intrigued with their movements."

Even though I knew this was one of John's practical jokes in the making, I could see that Jeshua was indeed intrigued. I watched carefully. The steps were not that difficult. I turned to John and smiled.

"Thank you, John. It's a wonderful idea!"

He looked a little taken aback, then smiled and clasped my hand briefly.

"Good for you, Magdalene. You'll do nicely."

I was to find out later the meaning to his cryptic remark, an acknowledgment of both my determination and my commitment to Jeshua and to my marriage.

The next evening's meal was much quieter. Most of the guests and entertainers had departed save one small band of local musicians. After the meal, I caught John’s eye and raised my eyebrows in a question. He smiled and nodded, then engaged Jeshua in conversation. I slipped unnoticed from the group and hurried to my room where I slipped into the costume I had purchased from the Nubian dancing girl. I finished dressing and was fastening the bells around my ankles, when Jeshua opened the door. I covered my face with the veil and motioned him to the cushion on the floor. When he was seated, I poured a cup of wine for him and then lit some of the candles. I passed by the window motioning to the group of musicians below in the courtyard who began playing. The music was soft and sensual and as I began moving to the age old rhythms, Jeshua smiled and drank deeply of the wine. As the music built in tempo, my movements drew me closer to Jeshua. I whirled and teased, dropping the attached scarves one by one. Each time he reached for me, I twisted away, teasing and tantalizing. Faster I twirled, closer and closer.

Suddenly his hand grasped my wrist and I fell clumsily into his lap. He laughed softly and gave me his wine to drink.

"Wherever did you learn that?" he asked.

"I persuaded one of the Nubian dancing girls to teach me

before the troop left today. Did my dancing please you, my husband?" I asked coyly.

"You know that it did, my love. I had no idea you could be such a tease. Promise me one thing."

"Yes, Jeshua?"

"Promise me that I am the only one who will ever see these most extraordinary talents."

"Are you sure you want to keep my talents hidden? I'm sure James and John would appreciate the effort it took to learn this dance."

"I'm sure they would, if they saw the results. But they won't see this remarkable demonstration of your ability to drive me wild with longing. This is for me alone."

He kissed me then, and drove all other thoughts from my mind.

* * * * *

Though all these things are clearly remembered, there is a problem with telling the world that Jeshua was not a celibate and serious religious scholar. For twenty centuries, the world has been told a story contrived to have the life of the man correlate with the teachings of the church designed to keep the masses subdued and controlled. The reality of the life Jeshua led, as I recall it, has little in common with the "only begotten Son of God" image that he has been painted with by organized religion. The fact that he was a husband and a father has only been alluded to in the past decade and then only as a theory.

To be honest, I was uncertain about my memories of this at first, for I, too, if you remember, was schooled in the "so far above mortal man as to be untouchable" myth. I continued writing and reading and was led to a book written by a woman who set out to prove that those who thought Mary Magdalene was not a harlot were mistaken. What she discovered was a preponderance of evidence to the contrary. The author is Margaret Starbird and her remarkable book is titled "The Woman With the Alabaster Jar".

When I was led to this book, I was at a point when al-

though I fully trusted the information given to me by the Guys, I was less certain about information that flowed from me when I wrote of those experiences. I picked up the book, read ten pages, and collapsed in tears of joy and relief. Finally, Mary Magdalene had been recognized and vindicated! The rest of the book was the same. I read a few pages and stopped to cry, read some more and cried again. It was such a redeeming and uplifting experience for me. I will always be grateful to the author and to the friend that directed me to it. Reading of the Forgotten Bride even now brings a surge of emotion and the urge to again weep tears of both sorrow and joy. I suppose I will always have mixed emotions when I recall that lifetime.

Though the memories of the marriage to Jeshua belong chronologically before the Baptism, that event is the first that I recalled in detail. Those details were so very crisp and clear that it was as though I was again at the river feeling the breeze and hearing the sounds of the people who gathered to hear Jeshua's cousin, John.

* * * * *

Chapter 8

We arrived at the river at midday. The sun was hot, but not uncomfortably so. Jeshua was already there speaking with a small group of friends, James and Lazarus among them. Jude and John were on the opposite bank of the river with another of the Zebedee brothers. I greeted John, who some called the Baptist, and hugged him. His smile lit up his face.

"Welcome, Magdalene. How are you faring as Jeshua's wife?"

"Fine, John. I am quite content, though it has been such a short time that I am still adjusting to it. You must admit Jeshua has a strong personality."

"And you do not?"

He threw back his head and laughed loudly. Then he looked into my eyes and his smile faded.

"What bothers you, Magdalene? Is this not the day that we have prepared for? Why is your heart troubled?"

"I am anxious for this to be over, but frightened also, and I'm not sure why."

"You will need great courage, Magdalene, and a great heart for the coming events. But these you have in abundance. We will all do what we have come here to do."

John kissed my forehead and smiled down at me. "Now I must return to the river. Watch carefully. Remember all that you will see this day."

John turned and waded back in the river. His mighty voice echoed through the river valley.

"Repent! Repent! The time of deliverance is upon us! Come and be baptized! Repent your sins and prepare your hearts to receive the Lamb of God. I baptize you with water and the word, but there comes soon one who will baptize with the fire of spirit, whose sandals I am not worthy to lace."

I stood there, held spellbound by John's words and the fiery delivery. Men and women began to enter the river and come before him to be baptized. His followers tried to form some semblance of order in the crowd, but the people heard John's voice and were drawn to the river, to the salvation and hope of deliverance that his words held.

I felt a hand on my shoulder and turned to see Jeshua beside me, watching John in the river.

"My cousin is a sight to behold, Magdalene. His words call to those who thirst for God's truth, those who know that there is more to God than is being taught by the priests in the temple."

"Yes, John is a gifted speaker; but I would much rather hear you speak of the Father."

"Is that because I am your husband, who loves you dearly?" he asked smiling.

"No, Jeshua. Because you speak of God as a loving Father, who has compassion and caring for his children, the kind of father mine was to me, and yours is to you, not the angry God that John speaks of who seeks only to punish those who disobey His will."

"John knows of this God, also, but he speaks to the people in a way that will attract their attention and open their hearts to the reality of God in their lives. We are each here to do our part, and John does his part exceedingly well."

"Yes, he does."

Jeshua and I stood for a moment watching the steady stream of people make their way to John's side to be baptized. I felt Jeshua stir and followed his gaze to see James step into the river from the other bank. His eyes met Jeshua's. I could feel the energy flow between them and I knew the time had come for Jeshua and James to take their place in the crowd.

Jeshua took off his cloak, handed it to me and smiled.

"Courage, my Magdalene. All is as God intends. The plan goes according to schedule."

"I'm frightened, Jeshua. Everything changes today. I can feel it."

"Don't worry, dearest. Stay here and watch. See the Glory of God made manifest in the world."

Then he kissed me gently, briefly. My heart wanted to hold him tight, for I knew that nothing would be the same. Our lives would be forever altered by the events of the afternoon.

I watched Jeshua step into the river and take his place in line. James also had joined those waiting for baptism by John. They both reached John at the same time. I was aware of John and James, the sons of Zebedee and my brother, Lazarus, standing beside me.

I held my breath as Jeshua and James knelt, side by side, in the gently flowing river. The sun sparkled on the water; the summer breeze blew through the trees and ruffled my hair.

Suddenly, the crowd quieted and all movement stopped. All eyes were fixed on the sight of the two brothers, so close in appearance, kneeling before the Baptizer. It was as if all those present knew of the importance of the moment.

In the stillness, I could hear the river flowing, the birds singing, and the occasional bleating of a sheep grazing on the hill. It seemed that time itself stood still and all the world waited, hovering on the brink with anticipation.

John looked down at Jeshua and James with a look of love so intense, so fiercely proud, that it took my breath away. Then he spoke to them in a quiet voice, gentle and loving, yet the tone of his voice sent a shiver up my spine.

"So here we are, cousins, here where the Father has brought us to do that which we were born to do. In truth, I should be kneeling before you both, for I am not worthy to baptize those who are Masters above me."

James smiled. "Were you not there, cousin, at our first initiation, and the second, and all the rest? Were you not with us at each lesson, in each temple, learning at the feet of all the masters from whom we received the wisdom of the Ages?"

John laughed softly.

"You know I was with you and Jeshua through it all, James."

"Then you know that we have each acquired the wisdom that we were meant to and attained the mastership for which we were destined. We are none of us above the other, but each here to do the Father's will."

"James speaks truth," Jeshua said. "And can we please get on with it? This water grows cooler, and if I catch a chill, I'll never hear the end of it from Magdalene."

The three men laughed together.

"She is quite a spitfire, isn't she, Jeshua?" said John.

"And I wouldn't have her any other way," replied Jeshua.

Lazarus put his arm around me and hugged me. "Quite a man, your husband."

"Yes, he is." I whispered. "He certainly is."

John dipped his cupped hands in the river and then let the water flow over the heads of James and Jeshua. The very air around the three shimmered with the energy and vibrated with a low humming. A golden white light surrounded the three.

"I baptize you in the name of the Father, who gives life to all." John's voice rang loud and clear throughout the countryside.

Suddenly a loud clap of thunder startled all present and a bright white light illuminated both James and Jeshua, a shaft of light from the heavens, and a voice said,

"These are my beloved sons. Well pleased am I in them."

Jeshua swayed slightly and both James and John reached out to steady him. James stood and helped Jeshua to his feet, then embraced both John and Jeshua in the hugs they had shared since boyhood.

"Thank you, cousin," said James. "You have served us well today and earned a place at supper tonight at Lazarus' house."

"Thank you, no. I feel the need to withdraw for a time,

to meditate in quiet. But I thank you for remembering me." He resumed baptizing the crowd.

Jeshua and James came toward me, climbing the riverbank. John went to help steady Jeshua, who appeared to be disoriented. We made our way to the house of Lazarus and Martha, my childhood home, where we were living until our own home was ready. I was becoming concerned about Jeshua. His disorientation was not improving. He seemed to be having trouble with coordination and had to be helped up the stairs to our room when we arrived at home. He didn't speak other than a hoarse "Thank you" to James and John. When they left, I closed the door and looked at Jeshua lying on the bed with his eyes closed. Martha knocked on the door and brought in a bowl of cool water and some soft cloths.

"I thought this might help. Do you think he suffers from the heat?"

"I'm not sure what's wrong. But I'll make sure he stays quiet for awhile. Thank you, Martha. That was very thoughtful."

I placed the bowl on the bedside table and smiled as Martha shut the door behind her. I dipped the cloth in the cool water, wrung it out, and placed the cool, damp cloth gently on Jeshua's brow. He looked pale to me, and when I placed my hand on this, I could feel him tremble.

I caressed his cheek, smoothed his hair and sat beside him until he slept.

I walked to the window and looked out toward the river, hearing again in my mind the words of John, the Baptizer.

I stood at the window for a moment remembering the sight of James and Jeshua kneeling in the river before John, the golden white light streaming around them. I knew that something had changed. Something was very different about Jeshua, something I couldn't quite put my finger on.

I suddenly felt his eyes on me. I turned from the window and saw that Jeshua had awakened. He looked at me with a strange intense look, then reached out his hand to me. My heart skipped a beat, then wildly pounded in my chest.

What was happening? Why this excitement and the

small sniggle of fear in my belly? This was my husband, the love of my life, the only man I had ever wanted, the one I had loved since childhood. Perhaps he was not my twin flame, but he was so very close to my heart that I could not even begin to imagine a greater love.

And yet, there was a tingle of energy in the room, a compelling command in his look, even though he had not spoken. His outstretched hand beckoned to me, and his clear blue eyes drew me like a moth to the flame. Slowly, I crossed the room to his side and reached out to him.

When our hands met, I felt a surge of energy pass between us and would have pulled away, but he held tightly to my hand and gently, but firmly, drew me closer until I sat next to him on the bed. I looked deeply into his eyes, puzzled by what I saw and felt. This was Jeshua, and yet, not Jeshua.

What a strange thing to cross my mind! How could it not be Jeshua? I looked more closely and again experienced the eerie feeling of someone else looking out at me through Jeshua's eyes.

He sat up and gently, almost reverently, stroked my hair, then touched my face with a soft caress.

"Ah, Beloved," he whispered softly, and leaned forward to kiss me. As our lips met, I again felt the surge of power between us.

My heart seemed to expand and I was overwhelmed by the rush of joy and love that suddenly filled me to overflowing. This was more than a physical or emotional reaction to this man I loved and with whom I shared my life. This was soul recognition on a profound level. I drew back and looked into his eyes. I could feel the tears on my cheeks, but my sole focus was on him. My mind wanted to deny the possibility of what my heart and soul and every fiber of my being knew beyond a shadow of a doubt to be true. Through some miracle of God, the soul of my twin flame, the soul created at the same moment in time as mine, the soul I had traveled with throughout eternity, this same soul now inhabited Jeshua's body. This beautiful soul now looked out at me through Jeshua's deep blue eyes with such love, such longing, that it took my breath away.

"Sananda?" I whispered.

He smiled and brushed the tears from my cheek with his hand, "Yes Beloved. I am Sananda, the one who loves you above all others. I am here with you again."

I touched his cheek, believing his words, yet doubting at the same time. How could this be? Why would this happen? What did this mean to me, to Jeshua?

Then I gasped. Where was the soul of Jeshua? As I opened my mouth to speak, Sananda chuckled softly and placed a finger on my lips. "Not now, Beloved", he said. "I can see all the questions in your eyes, and we will speak of all these things later, much later."

With that he pulled me firmly to him and kissed me. All the doubts, all the questions faded from my mind and I gave myself over to the sensations of again being in the arms of my twin flame. I had always experienced passion and fulfillment in Jeshua's arms, but the warmth of those same arms around me, the touch of those same strong gentle hands, the feel of those same lips pressed against mine, ignited feelings and emotions within me that were by far the most intense I had ever experienced. The merging of my aura and energy with that of Sananda, the only other soul in the universe that perfectly matched mine in resonance and vibration enhanced and expanded all the physical and emotional reactions and sensations. When at last we lay exhausted, wrapped in each other's arms, I found myself sobbing against him. Sananda held me close and murmured softly into my hair stroking and comforting me as one would a small child, and after a while, I fell asleep in his arms.

When I woke, it was dark. A candle burned on the bed-side table. I reached out to find only the pillow that had cradled his head. I looked up and saw Sananda silhouetted against the open window. I sat up in bed pulling the covers around me, suddenly shy. He turned to me and smiled. The soft glow of candlelight emphasized the blue of his eyes and the warmth of his smile. He came to sit beside me and took my hand in his, caressing it with his thumb. He smiled and gently kissed the palm of my hand. Energy tingled from the top of my head down to my toes.

"Are you hungry?" he asked. "Martha was kind enough to send fruit and bread for us, and there's a carafe of wine to go with it."

Sananda poured wine for us both and handed me a silver goblet. I sipped the wine but really didn't taste it. My mind was reeling with the events of the day and I had many questions that needed answers.

I took a deep breath and looked up at Sananda. He was sitting cross-legged on the bed facing me eating grapes. How could he appear to be so calm? My mind was spinning and somehow my ability to reason seemed to have shut down. I opened my mouth to speak and he held up his hand to stop me.

"I know, Beloved. So many questions! Perhaps I can answer most if I tell you what I know. Then you can ask questions if I leave anything out. Is that all right with you?"

I nodded. "As long as you understand that I will probably have five new questions for every one you answer."

Sananda laughed and tossed a grape into my lap. "Here, eat. Keep up your strength, dearest. You are going to need it," and he winked at me.

I reached for the bowl of fruit on the table. I laughed as I unwrapped a small loaf of bread, broke off a piece and handed it to him.

"Have some," I said. "If this afternoon is any indication, we'll both need to eat more."

Again he laughed. As he took the piece of bread from me, his hand brushed mine. The brief touch set my heart to fluttering and the way Sananda's eyes darkened showed that he was not unaffected by the contact.

"All right, start talking before I begin asking questions. You always say, or rather, Jeshua always says... This could be very confusing."

"Yes. It probably will be. From the beginning, then. I stepped into Jeshua's body, with his express permission and at his invitation, to assist him in the work that we have all come here to do. I could not begin to describe the process. From Spirit it was very simple. We planned this before Jeshua's birth and waited only for the right moment for me to enter. The merging of our two souls to inhabit one human body is something that is unique. There may be things we have not expected, such as the disorientation I experienced earlier today. That was a surprise."

I smiled wickedly. "For one so disoriented, you certainly recovered quickly."

Sananda laughed. "You are indeed a gifted healer, my love."

"But what of Jeshua? What happened to Jeshua?"

"Jeshua's soul is still connected to his body and will return to join me within a few days. He has returned temporarily to the etheric plane."

"Why did he leave at all?"

Sananda smiled and took my hand. "Did not Jeshua tell you I was coming? Did he not tell you who I was?"

"In a way, yes, he did. To be truthful, I'm not sure I really believed him. It all sounded so... bizarre, actually. Another master coming to share his body. And then he told me it would be you, my twin flame, who, by the way, stopped speaking to me as my guiding voice when I married Jeshua. Would you care to tell me the reason for your silence?"

"I stopped speaking to you for the same reason that Jeshua has absented himself for a while. So we can have privacy we desire for this reunion. I wanted also to give you and Jeshua privacy at your marriage. You needed time to focus on him alone. And I'm sure you didn't even know I'd left."

"Don't ever think for a moment that I didn't know. I can tell you the precise moment you left my side."

"Then tell me, my love. When did I cease to be your constant unseen companion?" he asked rather smugly.

"You left my side when Jeshua slipped the wedding ring on my finger. I felt a surge of love through my heart, and then a hole of emptiness formed that was not filled again until you took me in your arms this afternoon. Heart of my heart, despite my great love for Jeshua, how could you believe I would not notice your absence from my life?"

Sananda reached for me and pulled me into his lap, blanket and all. He wrapped his arms around me and held me close.

"Not being by your side for those months was the hardest thing I have ever done," he whispered softly.

I looked up into his eyes that were so filled with love for me.

"Promise me, Sananda." I touched his face caressing his check.

"Promise what, my beloved?"

"Promise you will never leave me again, no matter what the situation."

"I promise, dearest. Never will I leave you."

The next few days were absolute bliss. Having Sananda in the physical with me was heaven. We spent long hours in the garden talking or walking on the hill behind the house that over looked the river. We spoke in detail about the whys and wherefores of this very strange arrangement. We also decided not to share the knowledge of Sananda with any who did not recognize the change. My family thought we were just being typical newlyweds in spending so much time alone. We took most of our meals in our room, not only to avoid the change being detected, but because, in essence, we were in a honeymoon period. It had been nearly five hundred years since we shared physical life and after this incarnation, it would be another five hundred, more or less, before we would share physical existence once again. We were both determined to make every moment count. And we knew that when Jeshua's soul returned, we would all get down to the business at hand.

When the time grew near for Jeshua to return, to merge with Sananda and to again inhabit his body, I began to have real doubts as to my own ability to cope with the situation. I had been so lost in the mist of love and the euphoria of time again in Sananda's arms that I had not thought much about the implications of Jeshua's return.

As I wandered through the garden at dusk a few days after the baptism, I was suddenly beset by fears of Jeshua's reactions. I knew this had been planned on a cosmic level since well before Jeshua's birth, but I also knew that the conditions of the earth plane made results unpredictable, and since Jeshua was indeed living as human, he would be subject to all the emotional reactions that being human entailed. I was suddenly terrified. Would he look on these last four days as betrayal with another man?

The idea shattered the fragile hold I'd had on all the emotions that had threatened to overwhelm me. I sank to the ground and wrapped my arms around myself. Tears coursed down my checks and I rocked back and forth trying to bear the pain. I leaned forward as the tears turned to sobs, my control totally shattered. My waist length hair fell around me, hiding me from the world, allowing me to give way to my fears and doubts.

After long moments of uncontrollable sobbing, I became aware of a hand on my shoulder and the presence of someone sitting on the ground beside me. When my sobbing stopped finally and I was able to take a deep breath, I wiped the tears from my face with my sleeve and tossing my hair back, looked to see who had comforted me.

Sananda sat beside me rubbing my back, waiting patiently for the end of my emotional release. When I looked up at him, the tears began again. He pulled me to him, sitting me on his lap, cuddling me like a one would a child.

"Magdalene," he said softly, "whatever is wrong? What can be so terrible as to warrant all these tears?"

"Oh, Sananda," I said. "I got so frightened thinking of Jeshua's return. What if he thinks I've betrayed him with you? What ever will I do?"

He made a funny noise deep in his chest and then burst into laughter. I was so taken aback by this unexpected reaction that all I could do was stare open mouthed at him in disbelief. Then I became angry. How dare he make fun of my very real fear! How dare he!

I jumped up from his lap and stomped my foot in frustration.

"Don't you dare laugh at me, Sananda! It's not funny!"

That only made him laugh harder. I stomped my foot again and turned to go, but he grabbed my hand and pulled me back into his lap. I struggled briefly until I realized he was no longer laughing, but was nuzzling my neck.

"Magdalene, my love. Whatever made you believe that I would think you had betrayed me?"

I gasped as the words sunk in.

"Jeshua?"

I pulled back and looked into his eyes. The twinkle of laughter told me Jeshua had returned. What a confusing situation!

He smiled and touched my cheek. "Yes, dearest." he said, "I have returned to you and Sananda. I couldn't bear to be away from you any longer." He held me close and nibbled my ear gently. "Although I hear that you were well taken care of in my absence."

I looked up at him again. His eyes sparkled with laughter.

"What exactly are you referring to?" I asked icily.

"Don't bristle at me, Magdalene. Let me explain the situation, then you'll understand."

I nodded. "But don't patronize me!"

"Believe me, dearest, patronizing you never entered my thoughts."

I punched his arm. "See that it doesn't," I growled.

Jeshua chuckled again. "All right, my little wildcat, do you want to hear this?"

"Yes. Tell me what happened to Sananda? And this better be good."

"Yes, dear," he replied. "When we planned this before my birth, we weren't sure that we would be able to accomplish all we wanted in the time allowed. So we thought, if Sananda could walk in for a short time while we were getting things established, it would give us more power. There would be two fully aware Masters anchoring the

Light, accessing the wisdom and the teachings of Light, providing a more stable base for the Christ energy, the love energy to anchor. The trick was to find a way for Sananda's presence without involving a lengthy walk-in or the birth process. In this case, we considered that a shared experience with some kind of merging of consciousness would work best. So, the man you now see and feel is actually the merged consciousness of both Sananda and myself. Each of us has opened our minds to one another and allowed access to every memory. So, my dear, I have a very clear picture of how you occupied your time in my absence." He grinned broadly.

I felt the blood rush to my face and covered my eyes with my hands. "Oh, no. What must you think of me?"

"I think you are the most beautiful, alive, wonderful passionate woman I have ever had the pleasure of sharing this or any other life with. I feel very blessed to be your husband. Your husband, Beloved. There is no regret or shame to be had with anything that occurred. It was your husband you loved, my dear, whether Sananda or myself. There will be no question of this again, for we both share all in this life for as long as our consciousness, our souls, remain merged."

"How will I know which of you is speaking? How will you... how will we...? What name do I use?"

"Jeshua, dearest. No one will know of a merged presence unless they sense it. None outside the group is likely to do that. As for telling us apart, I'll speak in this high voice..." his voice squeaked, "and Sananda will speak with this deep voice."

I giggled as Jeshua voice went from shaky falsetto to deep booming bass. He and I laughed away the tension and relaxed into an embrace.

"As for the more intimate moments, Beloved," he whispered softly, "I'm sure if we try hard, we'll figure out how to manage that, too."

I lifted my face for his kiss and felt the combination of energies of the three of us meld. The result was dizzying and breathtaking in its intensity. I pulled away and gulped in a breath of cool air. I held on to him tightly waiting for the dizziness to pass.

"Oh, my!" I gasped. "Do you suppose it will always be like that?"

Jeshua started to speak, cleared his throat, and replied hoarsely. "I'm not sure. Perhaps we should try it again."

The stars spun wildly behind my closed eyelids and the earth tilted on her axis beneath me. I was aware of the feel of the ground beneath me and then the sensation of flying to the stars.

* * * * *

I woke to sunlight and birdsong and a tickling sensation on my cheek. I opened my eyes to see Jeshua's deep blue eyes sparkling with merriment. In his hand was a long blade of grass with which he was tickling my cheek. I had no memory of coming into the house, but was very thankful I woke in my own bed and not unclothed at the bottom of the garden, which was my last conscious memory of the night.

Jeshua leaned down and brushed my forehead with his lips. "Good morning, sleepyhead. Martha asks if you'd like to join us for lunch."

"Lunch! What time is it?" I jumped out of bed and flew around the room gathering my clothes and dressing quickly. "I promised Lazarus that I'd look at a new shipment of fabric and my new dress should be ready today."

Jeshua laughed. I looked at him. He leaned casually against the door, arms crossed and grinning at me.

"What are you laughing at?" I demanded.

"You, my dearest, bustling about as though you don't remember spending a good part of last night making love in the garden. I suppose this means the honeymoon is over."

I crossed the room and put my arms around his neck bringing his face close enough to kiss.

"Jeshua, my silly husband, don't you know by now that for us the honeymoon will never end?"

I was late for lunch. Again.

Chapter 9

Sananda's version:

You had been married for less than a year when word reached you of Mary's ill feelings toward you. You had little contact with her for you and Jeshua lived with your family at first since there was plenty of room. Mary was upset that you had taken Jeshua from her. You were not the shy, complacent daughter-in-law she desired who would sit at her feet and beg to learn her wisdom. At twenty, you knew much more than she did of the way of things, religion, politics and so on. She started tales based on her first sight of you in the marketplace flirting, disheveled, dirty. The word "whore" had not yet entered, but the questioning of your maidenly reputation had its beginnings in her words to others of her son's choice in a woman to wed.

Your awareness of the "mission" became clearer and you discussed much with Jeshua concerning the events to come. I began appearing to you in your dreams to prepare you for my merging with Jeshua. You spoke openly of the dreams with him and he told you plainly of the coming baptism and what it would mean to us all. He expressed his all too human fear that my presence would somehow change things between you, but you reassured him of your love and devotion.

Another source of contention with Mary was that Joseph developed the habit of dropping by in the evening to chat and share a cup of wine. Mary was needed at home with the younger children and did not feel as comfortable in your home as Joseph, so he came alone and often and stayed late. You and he sat often by the fire and talked of many things. Some of the conversations you shared with Jeshua were sparked by those of you and Joseph.

The day of the baptism, you were beside yourself with anxiety and anticipation. You stood at the water's edge watching as Jeshua approached John in the river. You heard his words, saw the bright light that engulfed Jeshua, felt the crackling of the energy as I merged with him. He swayed slightly, then was helped to the bank. You and John ben Zebedee helped him home while the Baptizer continued to preach to the crowd of the Light of God made manifest among them.

When we arrived home, you and Jeshua retired to your room and John returned to the Jordan. Jeshua napped briefly and you sat beside him wondering at what you had seen. Could it be real? Could the soul of Sananda now share life with Jeshua? As you wondered, you noticed that he slept no longer. He reached out his hand to you and drew you down beside him. You looked deeply, intently into the clear blue eyes, then knew without a doubt the truth of what you had been told and what you had witnessed. Sananda was indeed in the physical once more!

I will not tell you of our joining, the great passion once again known to us, but you have felt in your heart and soul the emotion of that sweet reunion. Jeshua's soul departed for a short time to provide a period of privacy. In truth, all three were hesitant about the intimacy of sharing a physical relationship after the merging, but the humor of the situation won out, and soon it was as though it had always been so.

* * * * *

Chapter10

I was glad to be able to travel with Jeshua. I usually did not accompany him while in Jerusalem due to the crowds that seemed to form whenever he stepped out into the streets. Though we never kept our marriage a secret not many knew of it outside the circle of family and friends. The few times I tried to walk along with him in town I was pushed and shoved by the those in the crowd desperate to touch him and speak with him. Jeshua could not be concerned for my safety if the job he was to do was to be accomplished as planned. I understood and traveled with him only away from the cities into the more sparsely populated areas. As the crowds dispersed in the evening, I spent much time with Jeshua sitting quietly or discussing the day's events and the teachings that he was dispensing to the small group of disciples.

There was another reason that I did not travel often with the group. Some of the disciples became jealous of my place within the group. First, I was a woman and a wife. My traditional place was at home tending to chores and bearing children. That Jeshua loved me and desired me by his side was an alien thought for most of them. The concept of a love so great that physical separation was unwanted had not been seen often in that part of the world with its arranged marriages. Once the inner group got to know me, most liked me and seemed to enjoy my company, but there were a few who longed for greater power and a place in the kingdom they thought Jeshua was prepared to fight for. They were afraid my presence would distract him from the task at hand, the liberation of Israel from the hands of the Romans and the restoration of the line of David to the throne.

Only one or two of them realized that the messages and teachings were not of the physical but of the spiritual. Nathaniel and Bartholomew were two of these, Andrew to a certain extent, but Peter and John, not at all. As the best friend of Jeshua, I would have expected John to see and hear the truth of Jeshua's messages, but John was envious of my place by Jeshua's side and felt that I had too much influence with him.

After the event at Mary and Joseph's, word had spread among the group of my abilities to channel the words of Spirit and Mary's remark about possession. While sitting apart one evening, I overheard some of them talking to Jeshua about it and they looked uneasily at me as though I was surrounded by demons. Jeshua looked amused at first and then concerned as he realized how serious they were about my being "possessed." I saw Jeshua take a deep breath and could almost hear him praying for guidance. Then he began to speak in a low voice that I could not hear. One by one the disciples left his side until he was alone. He looked over at me and smiled, reaching out his hand to me.

When I was seated beside him, he took my hand and looked into my eyes.

"They will never forget your name, Magdalene," he said. "I cannot know what they will say about you, but they will never forget your name!" And we laughed together in the evening shadows..

The next afternoon, many people gathered together to hear his words. Soon they were seated in a large semicircle on the banks of the river in a natural amphitheater. When they quieted Jeshua stepped onto a large flat rock near the river's edge and held his hands heavenward in blessing. His voice rang clear as he asked the blessing of the Father for all who gathered there.

"And I ask, oh. Father, that those who have ears to hear will carry the hidden meanings as well as the outward message in their hearts."

Jeshua then looked at those gathered on the banks and smiled.

"There once was a shepherd," he said, "much like King David as a boy, who discovered a black lamb among the newborn lambs of the flock. He thought at first to sacrifice it in the wilderness so the presence did not contaminate the rest of the flock. The lamb was smaller and weaker than the rest and the shepherd's next inclination was to allow the lamb die on its own as nature intended. But the shepherd, being of tender heart and loving all animals entrusted to his care, could not even allow the littlest lamb to be deprived of the affection and attention that he gave to all the flock. He held the lamb through the night and kept it warm next to his heart. He fed it soft bread soaked in warm milk since the lamb was too weak to nurse from its mother. As he sat through the night with this tiny lamb watching it struggle for nourishment and clinging tenaciously to life, he sang softly to it and watched the stars travel the night sky. He remembered the stories of David the King who began life as a simple shepherd boy and wondered if he, too, would have the opportunity to accomplish important things in his future.

Sometime during the long night, the shepherd dozed and fell into a dream in which an angel of the Lord joined him by the fire and admired the newborn lamb. The angel reached out his hands and took the lamb, then smiled at the tiny scrap of life.

'How blessed are you to have been given this gift from God. Surely this tiny black lamb will bring you luck and point the way to riches and happiness.'

'How can that be?' asked the shepherd. 'I have been taught that the black sheep brings only bad luck and ruination. I had even thought about letting the lamb die so it would not blemish the flock. How can you say that it will bring good luck?'

The angel smiled and gently handed the lamb back to the shepherd.

'The lamb that is different, that appears to bring shame and ruin to the flock, is the one that will willingly lead it to a better pasture and a newly discovered spring that flows pure from the heart of the earth. Can you say without question that this is not so? Would you take the chance that this lamb could be the saving of the flock one day? The Father's ways are often mysterious and will show themselves in the fullness of time. So have said the prophets."

The angel smiled again and the Light from his radiant countenance woke the shepherd from his dream.

'So the black sheep can be the salvation of the flock, the one that leads the rest to the purest water and the finest pastures. I believe that God has sent me a message this night. I will see what happens.'

The lamb gained in strength from that moment on and was nursing from its mother in a matter of hours. He grew strong and fine and was the pride of the flock, despite those who advised the shepherd to cast it off in order to avoid bad luck. A year later, the shepherd and the flock were set upon by wild dogs who nipped at the heels of the sheep and scattered them to the winds. The shepherd tried mightily to gather them back together and keep them safe, but three of the finest sheep, prized for their wool, were killed by the dogs and devoured. In the flight from the dogs, the shepherd noticed the black sheep disappeared behind a large boulder. Following, he discovered a passage through the rocks that led to a hidden canyon with a pure clear spring that bubbled from the side of the mountain and gathered in a crystal clear pool. In the canyon and up the sides of the mountain grew an abundance of fresh grass and vegetation that had apparently not been grazed in years, if at all. Wild fruit trees laden with fruit and edible plants grew in profusion and an outcropping of rocks made a perfect shelter for the shepherd and his flock.

The shepherd rejoiced in the discovery and thanked God, remembering the dream and the angel's words to him. They stayed in the canyon for several weeks until the time to shear the sheep arrived. The shepherd then took the flock back to town to sell the wool. The white wool fetched the highest price ever due to the luxurious feel and the brightness of the color. The black wool was purchased by a traveler in need of undyed black wool for the costly rugs which his family wove and made their livelihood. The high price of the black wool equaled the amount the shepherd received for the all the white wool sold that day. He and his family were able to expand the flock thus beginning the riches and abundance prophesied by the angel in the dream."

Jeshua looked out at the crowd gazing into the faces of each man, woman, and child with such love and compassion that I shivered in spite of the day's heat.

"Do not be hasty to judge from the outward appearance the value of another, for the value of the heart is known only to God. Had the shepherd followed the tradition and superstition of his friends and family, he would have missed the opportunity of riches that awaited him. As God treasures each and every one of his children regardless of outward appearance, so we should honor and value all, whether we discern the value at present or wait until the fullness of time to discover the hidden worth."

Jeshua stepped from the rock and stood next to me, his smile tender and gentle as he looked down at me. He stretched out his hand to me and raised me to my feet. Then he led me and the others back to the house of Samuel where we had been invited for the evening meal.

Chapter 11

Jeshua was in great demand for his teachings. Wherever he went he was asked for stories and to speak of the love of the Father that was so close to his heart and so absent from the writings of the prophets. People flocked to hear the positive messages of love and hope and the parables that led them to higher knowledge disguised in simple stories of everyday life. Many came to Jeshua hoping to be healed. Jeshua taught the disciples healing techniques that he learned during his travels to the far eastern lands. He also instructed me and Eena, who wanted to be as involved as much as Jeshua would allow. She would frequently dress in boy's clothing and tie her hair back, slip out of her house, and show up in the group of followers close to Jeshua. At first Jeshua sent her home so as not to worry their mother but as time went on without any remarks from Mary about Eena's escapades, he realized that Mary had little interest in Eena. She was not the meek, demure, and obedient daughter her sisters were and for that reason did not earn attention from her mother. Her father, on the other hand, admired her zest, determination and insatiable curiosity. These traits are the very things that she and I shared and that made us fast friends.

When she arrived at my door early one morning, I did not have the heart to turn her away. She had paid close attention to Jeshua's lessons on healing with the life force of the Universe and was ready to put it into practice.

I could not dissuade her from tagging along with the group and that is how Jeshua's sister ended up in the middle of a leper camp with the rest of us.

The lepers made their homes, if caves in the wilderness could be called homes, far from the towns. The families of the unfortunate victims brought food and clothing to them but once the signs of the disease were evident could not go near them or touch them again. This was heartbreaking for all concerned. Sometimes the families made the decision to move to the leper camp even though it guaranteed a certain, slow and painful death. There was no cure.

On this particular day we made our way to the leper camp not knowing exactly what we would find. None save Jeshua had ever visited the camp before and those who had accompanied him on his previous visit refused to go again for fear of possible contagion. Several of the group tried to keep Eena at a safe distance. She called out to Jeshua and me and he called her to his side. We both told her what to expect but the physical reality was overwhelming. The stench of rotting flesh was overpowering. She blanched and tried to take shallow breaths.

"Take a deep breath, little sister, and hold in your mind the fragrance of the blooms in Lazarus and Bethel's garden. Remember why we are here and focus on the task of easing the pain and suffering of these children of the Father." Jeshua placed an arm around her shoulders.

"Courage, little sister. The angels are with us as we do the Father's work here today. Do not fear the disease. We are protected from it."

"I am not afraid for myself, Jeshua. I am afraid of failing these poor souls. How can I hope to help so many when this is so new to me?"

"Concentrate on doing what you can for one at a time. Focus all your energy, place your hands gently on the shoulders, ask for the Father's blessings for him or her and bring in all the love of God that you can while with that one person. You will know when the energy has passed to that person. Give thanks to the Father and then give encouragement and a smile. Then do it again and again."

Eena smiled at Jeshua and stood tall, her doubts and uncertainties vanquished. She was determined to see it through and courageously walked with her head high and a bright smile fixed as we entered the camp.

Jeshua was immediately besieged by people wrapped from head to toe in strips of cloth and rags to hide the deformities from sight. In many cases the disease had affected the extremities and the person had lost fingers, toes, even ears and noses died and were sloughed off.

Eena saw the children, some of whom were still healthy and sound, and focused her attention on them. She started with a boy of about seven years, placing her hands on his shoulders and telling him to ask God for healing while knowing in his heart that God had already healed him. The hearts of children are trusting and pure and still very close to God from whence we all come. The boy closed his eyes for a moment, as did Eena, and then shouted in joy when on opening his eyes, saw that his lesions had disappeared. When he tried to thank Eena, she reminded him that she had done nothing but place her hands on him. He had asked God for healing and trusted it would happen. God had answered his prayer.

Jeshua looked at me and smiled as if to say," She learned well." That was the last moment we had to share a look until sunset when we wearily made our way back to town. Not all we laid hands on were healed. Jeshua explained that all have lessons to learn from the conditions of life and those conditions are healed when the lesson has been learned. There is no punishment in any physical condition of the body for the soul chooses before its birth into the physical body which conditions will best serve it on its eternal path to perfection. Those who received healing at our hands were those who were ready to break free from the chains of physical limitation that were self-imposed in order to show others the way.

We were physically exhausted and emotionally drained and devastated. There were so many that required help and so few of us who wished to try. We were bitterly disappointed in those followers who had lost faith in the Father's protection and would not enter the camp. A few helped the families on the outskirts of the camp but most who did not enter returned to town. The disappointment with those who left, the feeling of being overwhelmed with the sheer numbers of those needing help, and the degree of despair of those forced to live as cast-offs in order to remain with their loved ones touched us all deeply.

We spoke very little when we arrived home. We washed and changed our clothes sending them out to be burned. We tried always to keep the rest of our family from contagion. We then ate and fell into bed, too tired for anything but the shortest of "good nights." That was one of the times when the hopelessness of the situation, though lightened by Jeshua's presence and help, and the weariness of physical life hung on for days. Life in Palestine was far from easy.

Chapter 12

Though Jeshua and I loved one another intensely, life was not all sweetness. We had disagreements and occasionally even antagonized each other (in teasing, loving ways) for the sheer pleasure of making up when it was resolved. But the argument that occurred because of Mary was not playacting on anyone's part.

I occasionally traveled with the group to care for Jeshua and to feel a part of the active work, not just a bystander. Truth be told, I handled a lot of the tiresome details of the group, things that I was well trained to do. I learned much about the trade business from my father and Lazarus and knew who had the best goods for the best prices. Though Judas took care of the actual money, the purchases were usually ordered and delivered by the time he came with the funds for payment.

While traveling with the group, I kept a close eye on Jeshua to see that he did not allow himself to become exhausted. Between the zeal and passion for the work of both Jeshua and Sananda, there were days when he forgot to eat and did not rest as needed. Sometimes I had to gently take control and see to it that he ate a meal and stole away for rest. The inner group knew of my great love and devotion to my husband, but some of the larger group, some with no knowledge of the marriage, began to spread ugly, vicious rumors about my character and my reasons for traveling with Jeshua.

Mary soon heard these rumors and tales. She never really accepted me as Jeshua's wife but tolerated my presence with grace enough in front of others. Soon, however, the tales that were related to her developed into wild fantasies of my behaving "no better than a whore." I admit that I always liked people and liked the conversation and interaction of those who came to hear Jeshua speak. I spent time in the crowd talking with people, answering questions about Jeshua's teachings, and making them feel at ease. I was quick to embrace those in need of encouragement and never thought that my easy laughter and genuine caring could be misconstrued as anything other than compassion.

There was a day that Jeshua visited his mother alone, or as alone as Jeshua ever was, and she told him all the tales she had been hearing with a few embellishments of her own. Though I was not privy to the conversation, Eena overheard most of it and reported to me later that evening. Unfortunately, it was too late to prevent the outcome.

Mary pointed out to him that the work of establishing his claim as the long awaited Messiah would suffer if people had the impression that he had a less than perfect wife.

"Why does she follow you around like a common tramp? She should be keeping your home and bearing your sons. You have been married nearly three years and there is still no sign of a child. Is she barren, or does she not wish to spoil her figure by carrying a child of the Messiah? Jeshua, look at the impact this woman is having on those who follow you and listen to your words and wisdom. I beg of you, assert your husbandly rights and take her to task before she single handedly destroys all we have worked for all these years!"

Jeshua fumed but he kept his temper and soon departed. Because he said nothing against her hateful words, she assumed that he agreed with her and would take care of the problem. I, on the other hand, had no idea that there was a problem. Those closest to Jeshua and me knew how unfounded the rumors were and kept them from me so as not to cause us distress. When Mary summoned me to her home, I was glad to go. I had longed for the chance to feel closer to her and to change her opinion about me if I could. Jeshua's happiness was important to both of us and it seemed to me that a closer relationship between us could go far to see that happen.

Those hopes were quickly dashed when she greeted me coldly.

"I never approved of the match between you and my son," she began. "If I had my way, Joseph and Simon would never have drawn up the marriage contract. God himself has seen fit to designate Jeshua as the deliverer of Israel from the oppression of the Romans and the wife of the Messiah should be one who befits the station of that honor, someone whose reputation is untarnished and above reproach. Such a woman should not go traipsing around the countryside like a common camp follower with wild and unruly hair. You have been seen in questionable situations and I have had reports of your unseemly behavior with those of the group that accompany Jeshua on his travels. It appears that you are begging for his attention and the attention of any man in sight. How he has put up with your behavior is more than I can understand."

I was flabbergasted and too stunned to speak. I had no idea where these accusations came from but I could see by the look on her face and the hatred in her eyes that she believed every word of what she heard and was not interested in anything I might have to say in way of explanation. She turned to face me again and continued.

"Nothing can be done to change the fact that you are Jeshua's wife. You must change your manners and conduct yourself in a manner that will bring honor instead of shame to him. You should try to assist him in the work that he has to do and not hinder him by constantly following him around and getting in his way."

Mary smiled a cold hard smile, "Jeshua himself admitted to me today that your constant presence has been distracting. He is also appalled at the familiar way you behave with the group of disciples. When I asked him about your barrenness, he turned pale and left," she gloated. "I suggest you return to your home immediately and begin behaving like a respectable wife and less like a camp following whore!"

I longed to shout and scream at her and tell her exactly what I thought of her but my love and respect for Jeshua and his father made me keep my tongue. I asked her what Jeshua's reply to her accusations had been.

"Jeshua said nothing but I could see that he agreed with my wisdom in this matter."

Though the day was pleasantly warm, a layer of icy cold gripped my heart and soul. Jeshua had said nothing in my defense, not a single word against all the vile and vicious words of his mother. I was devastated, hurt beyond words. I don't recall leaving Mary or making my way back home. All I could hear were her hateful words and the gloating way she relayed Jeshua's lack of response. I was terrified that Jeshua believed her words without asking me for an explanation.

All through the late afternoon I replayed the conversation. The later it got the more fearful I became and the more fearful I became the angrier I got. By the time Jeshua arrived home shortly after sunset, I had worked my self into a frenzy. Though my mind knew to keep quiet and let him tell me in his own words what had occurred, my mouth seemed to take control.

"I was called to your mother's house today. She said some very cruel and hateful things to me and accused me of causing you shame and damaging the work you do. Then she gloated as she told me that she had spoken to you earlier in the day and that you spoke not one word in my defense. How could you have allowed her to speak so ill of me? Surely you know that all she said were lies!"

I waited for him to speak, to apologize for not taking my part and to hold me and make the hurt disappear.

"I have spent the afternoon speaking with James and John," he said quietly. "From the things they have observed, it appears that some of what she said to me is true."

"Did you not tell her how I take care of you and minister to your needs?" I asked.

"I did not feel the need to answer any of her words, especially since I have discovered the truth in most of them," he replied.

"She practically threw in my face that I have not yet conceived your child. Did you at least tell her that the time was not yet right for a child considering your work and the need for so much travel?" I asked.

"I could not tell her that we have decided not to have a child for a while. She would not understand our reasoning."

"So you let her think, at best, that I am barren. Or at worst, that I refuse to bear your child so I can continue tramping through the countryside, as she put it. How could you? How could you not defend me, or at least explain? You know she has never cared for me and has done all she can to come between us. You have heard her vile remarks to me and her insults."

"No, Magdalene, I have heard only your recount of that. She has never, in my presence, said anything that could be construed as hostile. She has always been polite and cordial to you. I do not know where all this comes from."

"And what of the rest, the stories about my behavior in the camp. Do you take her side there, too?" By this time I was nearly shouting. I was incredulous that he could think this was so unimportant.

Jeshua looked at me. For the first time in our marriage I could not read his expression, could not see the love for me in his eyes.

"I think, considering all that I have been told today, that you should remain at home for a time."

I felt as though a sword had pierced my heart, for never had we separated for any great length of time and the trip to Galilee would take him several weeks to months. My heart could not believe he said it so nonchalantly.

"When did you plan to leave," I asked quietly. That should have told him how hurt I was.

"Next week, "he said.

"Perhaps you should stay with John to help finalize the the plans and oversee the preparations."

"There is no need. John can see to it. Come to bed, Magdalene. It has been a long and taxing day."

I looked at him incredulously. How dare he think after all that, he could just take me to bed and pretend none of it had happened!

"I think it would be better if you helped John. From his house." Then the temper flared and my voice raised an octave.

"I cannot believe you stood there and listened to your mother talk as though I was a whore and did nothing to defend me! And then you asked the others for their opinions on my behavior. Jeshua, you have seen all I do and hear all I say to those who follow you. Never have you rebuked me or hinted that my behavior might be seen as inappropriate. Why now?"

"My mother pointed out that the way you are being seen by others may have an undesired effect on the way the work is perceived."

"Do you think she is right?" I asked.

He waited a long moment and stared at me. I refused to let the tears flow and stood proudly, the anger showing, the pain well hidden.

"I think it would be prudent to have you stay behind for a while so I can concentrate on the work at hand without you dragging me off to eat or insisting that I rest when there is still so much to accomplish," he said carefully.

I turned and went to the bedroom and returned with an armful of his clothing. I shoved it into his arms and stomped to the door, and threw it open banging it into the wall.

"Go to John," I said. "He will not nag you to rest when you are past the point of exhaustion. He will not remind you to eat when your stomach growls in protest of the emptiness within. He will go along with anything you desire whether it is in your best interests or not, for you are the very learned teacher and we are merely the dedicated followers. Go on! Walk until you are exhausted, go without food until you are faint. Speak to the crowds until your voice fails from overuse. He can do more for your work than I can. You obviously do not need me to help in the work that we have all come here to do. Now go!"

The tears began to fall. Jeshua walked to the door and stopped before me. He raised his hand to stroke my face in the familiar gesture but I turned from him trying to hide my tears. Jeshua let his hand fall in shock and sadness. Never before had I pulled away from his touch.

"I will go, Magdalene," he said. "See if you can conduct yourself like a dutiful wife until my return."

I slammed the door behind him and collapsed in tears.

Jeshua, having allowed his anger and blind faith in all his mother said color his words and actions, strode determinedly to John's. He did not hear my sobs or see my tears. He and the group departed for Galilee the very next day and when I made my way to John's to throw myself in his arms and beg his forgiveness, he was not there. I held onto my dignity until I returned home, then I gave in to the despair and the fear that he would not understand and would not forgive my hasty words to him.

The part about the child hurt me the worst for I longed with all my heart to bear his child, a child born of the love we three shared one for the other. Our joint decision had been to wait a while for the long journeys would not be conducive to pregnancy. I very seldom would hear of being left behind and none of us wanted to take any chances with the health of a baby. Until Mary's words, I had been content to place to the side my desire to bear Jeshua's children. Now that desire blazed forth within my soul and I could no longer deny the overwhelming need to conceive this child, and soon. Something within me knew that time was running out for my ability to accomplish this, to have a child conceived of the three.

That is, if Jeshua returned to me. I could only pray he would.

As the weeks passed, I began to lose hope and despair set in. The few people I saw could see the effects of my quarrel with Jeshua. At first I tried to keep up with the work in his absence but I had no appetite and I had trouble sleeping at night. Eena became concerned about the dark circles under my eyes and the paleness of my skin. The sadness in my eyes and demeanor was apparent to all who knew me and an indication that something was very wrong.

A month into the trip, Nathaniel, who had witnessed the changes in me, made his way to Jeshua in Galilee as had been prearranged. Nathaniel was to tell Jeshua of all that happened in his absence as was the usual case. When Jeshua inquired about my health, Nathaniel hemmed and hawed and tried his best to evade the subject as I had asked him to do. Jeshua wormed everything out of him and was appalled to discover that my health had been so affected.

He made plans to cut short the trip and return. As most men, he did not consider the quarrel to have been so important. He had seen me lose my temper, as had everyone within a mile's distance, but never before had it been directed toward him. He did not understand the depth of my pain or the betrayal I felt when he refused to defend me to his mother. He only knew that I had been deeply affected and was anxious to return to set things straight.

Chapter 13

He sent word that he would be returning to Lazarus' house on the way home. I decided that the home of Lazarus and Bethel was as close to neutral ground as there was. Maybe if we met in a semi-public place we would be forced to watch our words and not give into the anger that caused the quarrel in the first place.

I arrived at their home a full week before Jeshua's expected return. As they rushed out to greet me, I could see the surprise and concern on their faces as they got a good look at me. My hair had lost its sheen and I had lost weight that I could ill afford to lose. Bethel embraced me and held me a long moment until I could control the sudden tears. Lazarus also embraced me.

"My heavens, Magdalene," he said, "what on earth has happened. Have you been ill? Why did you not send for me?" My eyes again filled with tears and I looked to Bethel in a silent appeal.

"I'll take care of Magdalene, my dear," said Bethel as she swept me into the house. "Why don't you go to the shop and let us have a nice long talk. Have you checked the latest delivery yet? I heard Jacob say that he was unpacking it in the storeroom."

"I know when I have been dismissed," said Lazarus with a smile. "But I want to know what has happened when I return for supper."

"Yes, dear," Bethel answered. She took me to her room and listened sympathetically as I poured out my heart, and many more tears, to her. After she heard all the details, she hugged me to her to comfort me and then laughed softly.

"Magdalene, there are all kinds of misunderstandings that happen in a marriage. Whenever two people, especially those of passionate natures, share their lives on a daily basis, tempers flare, words are said unthinkingly and in haste, and these things happen. In the heat of the moment, words can be exchanged that cannot be taken back, words that cause hurt and pain, but seldom are these quarrels serious or lasting. When two people love one another as much as you and Jeshua, then even a serious disagreement can be worked out. Please don't cry any more. He is due back in a week. How will he feel to see you looking thus?"

"Oh, Bethel, I wish I had come to you right away. You always give me such good advice. Have you and Lazarus ever quarreled?" I asked.

"Quarreled? Oh, my dear, we have had some spectacular ones! Several years ago, we had a misunderstanding, I can't even remember what about now, but I said something and he said something and before long I was screaming like a fishwife and throwing crockery at his head. I just missed him, luckily. He objected loudly at being the target. It was a real mess." She shook her head remembering.

"What happened?"

"Why, we kissed and made up, of course. Some very delightful making up, if I recall correctly. That is how we got our little Andrew. So some quarrels can have very happy endings. So it will be for you and Jeshua."

"Do you really think so, Bethel?"

"Absolutely, my dear, just wait and see."

I knew then that somehow Jeshua and I would come through this and I vowed I would never let my temper control my good sense again.

The next four days passed slowly. I grew even more restless and nervous and my pacing back and forth tried her patience. Finally, she sent me to the market to purchase figs that she did not really need or want just to get me out of the house and out from under her feet. As I walked into town I recalled the day that Jeshua returned home from his travels abroad, the day that he and Joseph asked my father for my hand in marriage. I remembered the joy of that day and vowed to have that joy with Jeshua again.

I reached the market and saw a brightly colored stall belonging to newly arrived traders from the East. I browsed through their treasures and saw an exquisite little alabaster jar filled with sandalwood ointment. Jeshua and I both loved the smell of sandalwood for it brought back memories of our time in Egypt. Even though I bargained with the traders for some time, the price we agreed on was still a costly one. But I felt it well worth the price and paid for it with some of the money left to me by my father.

I tucked it into a pocket hidden in my cloak as a present for Jeshua. Just the feel of the jar lightened my heart a bit and I returned to the house in better spirits.

When I neared the house, however, the crowd at the front gate told me that Jeshua and the inner group had arrived from Galilee. I realized that I was in my usual state of untidiness from walking in the breeze without a veil as it was tied around my waist, and ducked around the back so as not to be seen. I slipped in the back door and stole up to my room to wash and change. The longer I took to calm my nerves, the more nervous I became about the meeting.

I slipped down to the kitchen to see if Bethel had any inkling as to Jeshua's feelings.

"All will be well, Magdalene," she said smiling as she oversaw preparations for the evening meal. "He is waiting alone in the library for you. Go to him."

I quietly slipped into the library and found him dozing in a comfortable chair. His face was tired and worn and he, too, had lost weight. His hair was pulled carelessly back and tied with a cord, not his usual neatly groomed appearance. Then I saw his feet. He had obviously walked far and fast for there were scratches from thorns and blisters from the straps of his sandals.

I hurried to the kitchen and got a bowl of water and a soft cloth with which to wash his feet. I knelt beside him and gently removed his sandals. He was so weary and slept so soundly that he hardly stirred. I gently began to wash the dust from his feet and cried over the pain he must have endured, my tears mingling with the scented water. Jeshua woke but said nothing for a moment as he watched me tenderly ministering to him.

Unknown to either of us, Andrew and some others of the inner group had come to the doorway and silently witnessed our reunion. When I looked up and saw Jeshua tenderly watching me, I burst into sobs and embraced his feet, too ashamed to meet his eyes. He leaned forward and placed his hands on my shoulders.

"Magdalene, please," he said softly.

I cried all the more, then realizing that I had forgotten to bring a cloth with which to dry his feet, unbound my hair and gently dried his poor aching, injured feet with the shimmering mass of hair that he so loved to touch and feel around him. He grasped my arms and raised me to his sit in his lap. We held each other tightly, apologizing for the words spoken in haste and the anger towards one another. Then he kissed me and we were both lost in each other. Neither heard the door discreetly shut.

Somehow the story of me drying Jeshua's feet with my hair spread quickly and we were greeted with smiles as we emerged a time later from the library. Later that evening we sat again in the library enjoying the company of family and friends and the closest of he disciples. I sat at Jeshua's feet where I frequently sat to be as near as possible. As the evening wore on and all but the closest to us had gone to bed, I pulled the alabaster jar from my pocket and gently applied the healing ointment to Jeshua's wounds and bruises. The scent of sandalwood filled the room.

"Thank you, my love," said Jeshua softly. "It is not only the ointment that heals and soothes. Your touch heals my heart and soul."

I looked up and smiled at the look of love in his eyes. My heart lightened and I knew that we were all right. Then Judas spoke.

"That is a very expensive ointment, Magdalene. You should not have spent so much money on it. Think of how many of the hungry and poor we could have helped with the money."

Jeshua looked at Judas with a hard look.

"The poor and hungry will always be among us," he said, "but I will not always be here. This act is that of a loving and devoted wife who is the heart of my heart and the song of my soul. I will not have her denigrated by you or anyone else. You cannot know what she has endured because of me and her devotion to me."

Judas stood and looked scornfully down at me.

"My pardon, Magdalene." He took his leave and disappeared into the night.

Later that night in the privacy of our room we spoke openly and frankly about all that had gone on, including the conversations with his mother that started it all. The rumors and innuendos were discussed and explained, the words and tempers freely forgiven. And sometime that night a child was conceived, a child created of the deep and abiding love of Jeshua and Sananda for Mary Magdalene, and she for them.

Chapter 14

Jeshua and the disciples traveled to Samaria and on to Galilee several weeks later. I elected to stay with Lazarus and Bethel for several reasons, one being the hope that I had conceived the child we both now wanted. I certainly was not about to take any risks with the pregnancy. Suddenly, an uneasiness had descended on us and a feeling that time was running out. The decision had been arrived at by all three to conceive a child the night of the reconciliation after the quarrel. When my body began to show the subtle signs of pregnancy, I decided to play it safe and remain home for the three to four weeks that the trip would take.

I busied myself with the household chores that were necessary even though I had no real interest in them. Domestic bliss was always a contradiction to me, especially when Jeshua was home to provide more interesting things to do. Whenever he was home the house was filled with people and I gladly turned over the household chores to the housekeeper or whoever else would see to things so I could sit at his feet. As long as I could sit by him, touching him occasionally, listening to his words, and watching his face as he taught, I was content.

The trip to Galilee took longer than anticipated. I was not worried, though. I would know in my heart if something was wrong. Meanwhile, in Bethany, Lazarus was driving himself at the shop trying to get as much done as possible for the upcoming Passover holiday. He planned ahead for the time and had ordered many new fabrics and other items for the newest additions to the Roman community in Jerusalem. He was one who worked long hours and too hard, to Bethel's eternal frustration. He focused on the business and managerial side of things and was not much interested in the spiritual aspect of life. He listened often enough to Jeshua's words and respected him for his wisdom and education, but Lazarus was a practical man used to thinking more of providing for his family, which increased every year or two, than the Kingdom of Heaven. He attended the temple services and did what was required of him as a Jewish man in that time and place, but his heart was not in it. It was habit and tradition, nothing more.

Lazarus worked late into the night much of the time at the books, trying to make better bargains, and to establish better trade routes and alignments with the caravans that regularly came through Jerusalem. Whether in the office or the warehouse or in the study at home, he spent much of his time with his head in the business.

About the time that Jeshua was expected to return, he discovered that someone had apparently been stealing from the stores of goods that were kept in the warehouse. He noticed that only small things were missing and thought perhaps one of the many young children sent to beg in the streets had found a way into the warehouse undetected. He was determined to find the culprit and end the thievery. He spent four or five nights sitting in the dark in the warehouse in an attempt to foil the thief. The rain did not fall frequently, but this particular week it seemed not to let up. Lazarus sat wrapped in his wet cloak, never thinking he might catch a chill but his resistance was low due to the lack of rest and his habit of forgetting to eat when his thoughts were otherwise occupied.

The fourth night of his vigil was successful. He surprised the boy and caught him in the act of snatching a small golden box chosen for its small size. When Lazarus apprehended the boy he discovered the act was one of desperation. The boy's father had been killed in a skirmish with the Roman soldiers and his mother lay ill and unable to pay for food or medicine. The boy had been stealing for weeks to try to keep the small family supplied with food.

Lazarus' good heart could not turn the boy over to the authorities. Instead, he gathered food from the stores and medicine that he thought might be helpful and accompanied the boy home.

What he saw there broke through the gruff facade he wore. For the first time, he saw how much of the Jewish population lived in Jerusalem, the poverty and the scarcity. Yet there was such faith in the mother that God would provide that he was moved to tears. He saw to it that the family had a warm fire, a hot meal, and the services of a physician.

He wandered home that night through the rain lost in thought, realizing for the first time the words of Jeshua that rang true; he was his brother's keeper. If he, who had the resources to reach out to his fellow man, did not, then who would? Too long he had lived in the narrow vision of the world boxed in with the material focus that running a very successful business entailed. By the time he arrived home he was soaked to the skin and chilled to the bone. Bethel made him soak in a hot tub until he stopped shivering and then tucked him into bed, feeding him hot stew and warmed wine and listening to the pathetic story of the child who tried to provide for his family. It was the first time Bethel had seen him cry. They held and comforted each other through the night.

By morning's first light. Bethel knew he was ill. His skin was flushed and warm and his eyes were glazed with fever. She called for the physician and roused me from sleep. The two of us managed to keep him sponged and gave him water as often as he could drink it. I knew that his illness was very serious so I quietly sent a servant to fetch Jeshua. He had left me a plan of his travels so I had a good idea where he might be and mapped the way to find him on his return trip.

The servant found Jeshua and the disciples a little more than a day's journey away and informed him of Lazarus' illness. He gave Jeshua the message and my letter telling of how Lazarus had become ill and how serious the condition had become. Jeshua did not set out at once. He decided to wait. He knew what would happen and the opportunity it would present. He elected to let the illness run its course. He stayed and continued the teaching.

Three days later, when he received word of Lazarus' death, he and the disciples packed up and returned to Bethany. Those three days were a nightmare for me and for Bethel. I was in a daze. I wandered around, not really focused on the events yet functioning and performing all the required duties. Martha came from Jerusalem and mourned with Bethel as was the custom. I found myself comforting the children and tending to their needs, which suited me more than the public mourning. I also could not bear to be asked one more time of Jeshua's whereabouts or the reason for his conspicuous absence.

When we heard of Jeshua's impending arrival, I did not run to meet him as did Martha, Bethel and the others but stayed with the younger children in the house. Shortly after his arrival, Jeshua sent for me. I had thought to berate him for his absence but one look at him, at the grief in his eyes and the weariness in his face and I could not. I reached my hand to his face in the familiar gesture and then held him to me. After we had gained a small measure of comfort from one another, he asked to be shown the grave. The small party of family and friends showed the way to the same place my mother and father had been buried so many years before.

Jeshua placed his hands upon the stone sealing the crypt and openly wept. I stood close beside him, my arm around him and leaning close, giving him all the comfort and love that I had to give. When the worst was over, he wiped his face on his sleeve impatiently and stepped back several steps. He held my hand tightly then called for the steward.

"Roll the stone away from the entrance," he said.

I gasped with all the others at the strange request.

"Jeshua," said Martha," Lazarus' body has been interred these three days. The dampness and the heat....the stench will be overpowering! What can you be thinking?"

Suddenly Bethel's knees gave way and she collapsed into Martha's arms.

"Magdalene! Help me!" Martha called.

She and I helped Bethel into the house and settled her in the library. Then I returned to the grave, arriving just in time to see the steward and his helpers roll the huge round stone from the entrance of the tomb. The spectators gasped in disbelief as Jeshua advanced toward the entrance and called out in a loud voice.

"Lazarus! Lazarus, arise!"

Some thought the sudden grief had affected his mind and that he had not accepted the fact of Lazarus' death. How could Jeshua think he could command him from beyond the veil? Again, Jeshua called to him in a loud, commanding voice.

"Lazarus! Come forth! Come back to us so the will of the Father may be known and his mercy shown to all here present. Lazarus, come forth! "

For several long moments there was no sound, no sign. Then the sound of muffled footsteps came from within the open tomb. For a moment the significance did not register, then suddenly, a wrapped and shrouded hand grasped the rock and Lazarus struggled to exit the tomb.

"Help him!" Jeshua called to the servants. "Loose his wrappings."

As they did so, Lazarus covered his eyes from the harshness of the sun and those present murmured in disbelief at the evidence before them. Martha approached and touched him gently, then threw her arms around him with a glad cry. He embraced her and then looked at Jeshua.

"I was in a place of great peace and love, "he said hoarsely, "and then I heard you call to me. I could not disobey your command, Master."

Jeshua embraced him.

"My brother, the glory of God has today been seen here. Welcome back."

I, too, moved to his side to embrace him. Then Lazarus staggered and would have fallen if not for Jeshua's support. The servants hurried to help Lazarus into the house and Martha hurried to tell Bethel the glad tidings before she was confronted with the sight of her recently departed husband reclining in their bed. The rejoicing was long and heartfelt that night.

Those present spread the word and it soon reached the ears of the Sanhedrin and the Pharisees. It was the one event that, in their eyes, determined the fate of the blaspheming teacher in the hearts of those in power. Teaching of the power of God was one thing; a demonstration of that power and the reversal of death was quite another. The rumor of a hoax was quickly spread as the Sanhedrin tried to control the damage. Those who had seen knew the truth. Those who had not chose sides based upon their loyalties.

Lazarus recovered in time for the Passover celebrations three weeks after Jeshua's return and his remarkable miracle of calling Lazarus back from the grave. By that time, the pregnancy was far enough advanced to be confirmed and Jeshua, Sananda, and I rejoiced in the knowledge that we three had begun a new life together.

Chapter 15

Mary had focused her entire life on the goal of declaring Jeshua's blood right to be the King of the Jews. She had planned his coronation in her mind determined to have it rival that of King Solomon of old. Jeshua had these things drummed into his head from birth, the way his mother had been trained by the Essenes and chosen on the stair by the angel Gabriel and announced as the chosen to bear the Messiah. Mary told the story often to any who might be able to assist in her plan for Jeshua. She told Jeshua often about the traditional signs of the Messiah's birth. Isaiah spoke of a young girl who would bear the child, a child of the lineage of Jesse and David the King. She was convinced, like so many tired of Rome's oppression, that the long awaited Messiah would defeat the Romans and restore independent rule in place of the puppet king, Herod.

Although Jeshua knew that his mission was to teach about the spiritual aspects of God, he also knew that if people believed in the possibility of a physical world messiah they would be more likely to listen to his words and in listening, they might open to the truth of the spiritual world within. And so when the time was ripe, he chose to use certain symbols to remind people that he was indeed the promised one.

Jeshua and I discussed the importance of timing of certain events that would bring to the attention of followers and the populace in general that Jeshua was shunning the role of physical Messiah to embrace the spiritual. If it had not been shown that he was of the line of David and qualified to sit on the throne had circumstances been different, then the whole point of the entrance into Jerusalem would have been non-existent. The whole thing was carefully planned and executed by the inner group. Those who did not quite understand or accept the premise that Jeshua was the spiritual Messiah thought perhaps that he had finally come around to the logical way to proceed. Those who knew the truth and the intent kept their own counsel and prayed for the best.

By this time things had gotten so out of hand on several fronts that we three pretty much knew the way things would go. Although we tried not to dwell on the matter, we suspected that an execution of some kind was in the planning stages by the Sanhedrin. We expected it would be a stoning or some other kind of Jewish execution. Roman law, being as it was, and the courage of the Sanhedrin being non-existent when it came to defying Rome, we should have been more prepared for the way it turned out. Perhaps it was for the best, however. Forced to deal with the events as they occurred, we had no time to waste energy on anticipating what would come next. Once begun, the momentum gave us little chance for planning, though from Spirit, Michael and the other archangels had all in readiness and took over the preparation stage. Michael was the one who contacted Joseph of Arimathea and stayed in constant contact with us advising and encouraging, as he does in every physical incarnation.

When Jeshua asked for the donkey on which to ride into Jerusalem, he proclaimed his rightful heritage as David's heir to the throne of the Jews. He sent one of the disciples to Lazarus' house for the donkey, which had been tied outside in front of the house in preparation. I watched from a window and then followed for a short distance. I was apprehensive about the plan and was worried it might backfire in some way. When I saw the crowd begin to form and heard the singing, I knew it would be all right and I returned to Lazarus and Bethel's to wait for Jeshua's return.

Eena, dressed in boy's clothing, accompanied the crowd. Jeshua knew of her presence and assigned Simon, to watch out for her. As the procession made its way into the city, it attracted more spectators and participants. By the time the reached the gates of the Temple, there was a throng of singing and exuberant followers waving palm branches and praising Jeshua, thanking God for the presence of the Messiah. That was the thing that angered the Sanhedrin and the Pharisees. That they considered to be blasphemy. They preached the Messiah that God promised to deliver the Jews from bondage, but they believed not, not even in a physical Messiah who would release Palestine from the Romans. They had no such childish hopes and were content with making their physical world as comfortable as possible.

The temple priests insisted that the coinage paid for the animals to be sacrificed be that of the Temple. This involved changing the local coin for that of the Temple, at a rate set by the Temple priests, of course. So the Temple made money on the changing of coins to the Temple coin and on the sale of the animals and birds to be given in sacrifice. The money was not to help the poor or those in need but added to the already well-lined pockets of the Sanhedrin and the Pharisees. Each of the groups of priests had a stake in the money making game and none wanted to see the profits reduced. They did not see the logic behind the arguments to do away with the tables and felt they were providing a service to all who came to worship. Where else, they reasoned, would the visitor to the Temple in need of a sacrifice to the Lord be able to purchase a bird or lamb that would be pleasing to the Lord and fit the requirements for sacrifice that had been set down by Moses and Aaron as given by God Himself? The very question of the need for a sacrifice at all was not addressed as they were in the mind set of "this is the way it's always been done." There were also booths in the Temple's outer courtyard that sold tourist souvenirs, for the trip to Jerusalem was one that pilgrims made only once, in the case of those Jews living at a distance from Jerusalem. The trading within the outer courtyard was fast and furious on that day.

The entrance of Jeshua and the band of followers into the temple caused quite an uproar. The singing continued and brought to a halt the business of the booths as those engaged in business hurried to see what the commotion was about. When those in charge confronted Jeshua about the noise and commotion, there was a discussion that further disrupted the orderly, or disorderly rather, state of things. Slowly, things returned to normal and the visitors returned to the booths to complete their transactions. The singing stopped but those who followed Jeshua into the Temple now gathered around him to hear him speak. The noise of the business being conducted rose to a din that made having a conversation impossible. Jeshua stood on the stairs with the crowd at his feet but they could not hear his words for the noise of the merchants hawking their wares.

Finally, he had all he could take. His temper was not something that was unleashed often, but once uncaged was a mighty sight to behold. In this case the frustration of all that had gone on and the inability to really reach the minds of most with the true message helped to fuel it. The uncertainty of things also played into it, for although we all felt that something would snap soon, we did not know exactly how that would come about. It was like waiting for the second shoe to drop. Although Sananda did not like to admit it, his temper, when raised in righteousness, was also a mighty thing to behold. It was a case of "righteous indignation times three."

So there were the two of them who had been so gentle and loving and kind to all who came to Jeshua for assistance, healing, and teaching, having reached the limit as far as the manipulation of the priests was concerned. Jeshua's temper flared and Sananda agreed it was time to show them the full fury of the Father's wrath with the continued spiritual expression of his people. It was a sight to see, I was told. I heard of it later when they returned to Bethany under cover of darkness. Jeshua's words were remembered and recorded. What followed after his very loud words to the priests was something not seen before.

Jeshua overturned the table of the moneychanger nearest him and then the cage of birds behind him, setting them free to soar to the skies. Those with Jeshua first watched in open-mouthed amazement, then the frustration of years gave vent and others followed Jeshua's example. Those who had set up small private booths were left untouched. The booths owned by the Temple were destroyed. The followers fled when the Temple guards were called out and Jeshua was spirited away through the crowd with a cloak thrown over his head.

Eena ran back to Lazarus' house before the others who took a longer route home, and described it all to me and Lazarus, laughing as she impersonated the priests and Jeshua. Jeshua was not as lighthearted about the incident as Eena, for he knew that repercussions were sure to follow.

Chapter 16

From Sananda:

The memories you share point out the humanness of Jeshua, not the divinity of the legend that was manufactured. Paul and Peter and the organized church made so much of the divinity that the reality of why the words were said and why the human body chosen slipped by. The point of becoming human was to show the reality, the possibility of each and every man, woman, and child to actively communicate with God, with Spirit, without the intermediary of priest or any other. No one is held from the bosom of the Father or Mother. No one is made to seek another to go before, to prepare a way or a message. Each soul is always in communication with the Father and with the many in Spirit who help and assist, guide and protect. This is the message that Jeshua and I tried to present to those who heard, but the message was perverted and distorted through the beliefs and perceptions of those who heard the words and related them to others.

Paul's discourses on celibacy and the ordaining of women is a case in point. He used the name of Jeshua as a banner to project his personal beliefs and solutions. Those who heard him believed that Jeshua's feelings were along the same vein. Nothing could have been farther from the truth, as you know. Those who remember those days in their hearts and souls, and there are very few, regardless of the stories, recall the very active participation of the women in the early church and in the group in which Jeshua and I traveled. Paul's exposure to that was very limited and the facts he recalled (The Messengers) were not of the normal times and travels but of the exceptions and special circumstances.

Your presence (Magdalene) was not noticed for he was not accustomed to the presence of any woman as being important. You had a way of mingling with all, answering questions and relating our words to the women and to those who had difficulty understanding the stories. You were quite a figure to watch as you moved unobtrusively among those gathered to listen. Always my eyes sought you out in the crowd to see what kind of impact the teaching made. You would smile and nod slightly to indicate the message was understood and well received by the crowd, or shake your head slightly to show that greater clarity or a different approach was needed. Always you gave great encouragement, support, and great love to us both. How could you not? We were terrific!

Your concern touched my heart and Jeshua's as you saw the divisions become more apparent between those who heard the teachings on a spiritual basis and those who heard only from a physical perspective. Your intuition, and the murmuring of our beloved Archangel Michael in your ear, helped to save us from difficulty on more than one occasion.

It was James who decided to make a try for the throne, to present the physical Messiah, not the spiritual one. Mary was not the shy, demure thing that Paul recalls, at least after Joseph's death. It was he who kept her behavior within acceptable parameters. She pushed and maneuvered all she could to force Jeshua into action, as she did at the wedding with the water and the wine. It was at her pressuring him that the manifestation was done. He had not yet begun teaching and I had not yet arrived, but she did not know of the plan for the merged years and was not patient enough to let things unfold as they would. Had she been more mindful of the spiritual rather than the physical, she would have realized much sooner that the scenes she saw played in her mind of glory and honor were only the desires of the ego, not the way of our mission. The awareness of the plans was not brought clearly into play until the baptism.

Jeshua was still searching for the direction of his teachings, still trying to integrate all the wisdom that he had gathered from the far comers of the world in his teachings. My arrival and the merging of our minds and souls brought to his consciousness the mission's plans and the probable events and outcomes. When the possibility of the crucifixion became apparent, which was far earlier than you were aware, he went through a period of depression and withdrawal. This occurred during travels with the disciples when he withdrew for prayer and meditation. It was a very difficult time for Jeshua for he knew the body might not survive and the damage that would cause to your life and emotions he did not desire. For several days, he and I were in constant communication with Archangel Michael and others in Spirit as we discussed all the possibilities and outcomes. You would have been impressed with the contingency plans that we discussed, discarded, and reevaluated.

We tried to look at all the options and possibilities and to anticipate the events that might occur. The free will of the other participants, however, is what took us by surprise. We could not see within the hearts and minds of those who were determined to make an end to all that Jeshua tried to do. Although the modern world looks on Jeshua as the gentle shepherd, the man who loved children and took them to his embrace, (and you recall clearly how much we both did), Jeshua's message was the most radical heard in centuries. Here was a Jewish rabbi, a student of the Torah and learned man of all religions of the planet, encouraging men and women to think for themselves, to follow their hearts and their inner guidance, to bypass the temples and the priests and all the formal dogma of centuries of Israel and to go directly to the Father. It was heresy, pure and simple! And the very best way for mankind, then and now.

It's a shame that what Jeshua and I said then was so distorted and twisted in the years that followed and that it took so long for mankind to again open to our words and the possibilities of free will and direct communication with Spirit. You have always known the truth and have railed against the words of those who stated the only way to the

Father's heart and ear were through the voice of another, be it saint, the Mother, or Jeshua himself. As you record the events of Palestine and your life with Jeshua, do not forget the good times, the laughter, the fun, the jokes and the closeness we all shared. Recall the adventures we had as we upset the social applecart of the day by consorting with "thieves, sinners, and whores!" It was not to prove that we had to "save the sinners", but to show that in the eye of the Father/Mother, all are equals and deserve to know the truth of God's love for all. This above all is the truth that should be recalled.

* * * * *

The part of the lifetime as Magdalene that I put off looking at as long as possible was the crucifixion. Having relived a portion of that horrible time in regression, I was in no hurry to see it in the detail that I knew I would be shown. Yet, this was part of the enormous emotional burden that I had carried in from that lifetime and was immersed in the karma that I needed to resolve. The emotional intensity was my Higher Self's way of ensuring that I would look at that lifetime and then complete the tasks that would finally release me from the heavy burden that I had carried in my soul for two thousand years. I chose a weekend to devote to the project of writing the event in detail and prepared my wonderful and supportive family for the probability of many tears and much emotional release. They promised privacy when I desired it and support when I needed it, and so in a beautiful bright Saturday morning, I sat at my computer to remember and record the events surrounding the crucifixion.

Chapter 17

I was roused from sleep by the sound of someone pounding on the front door. As I grabbed my robe and pulled it around me, I heard the door being opened and the frantic hushed whispers of voices in the entryway. When I reached the hall, I saw Mara with a lighted candle in one hand and her other arm around a distraught and weeping John ben Zebedee.

"What in the world is going on?" I asked, and moved to take the candle from Mara.

John's face showed a bleakness and despair that I had never thought to see on one so filled with the joy of life. Tears streamed down his face and he struggled to find composure enough in which to speak.

"Magdalene," he sobbed, "they have arrested Jeshua. He is on the way to the court of the Sadducees as we speak. After the Passover supper tonight, long after you and the families and Eena had departed for home, he and I went to Gethsemane with some of the twelve. He had been sent word to meet Judas there. He felt the need for quiet meditation and asked if I would accompany him. After meditating for a while, I fell asleep. When I awoke an hour later, Jeshua spoke to me of all that has gone on with the Pharisees and the Temple."

I turned to John, who wiped his face on his cloak and leaned against the wall for support.

"Tell me what happened, John," I urged.

"Judas was convinced the time had come when Jeshua must move against the Pharisees. The scene in the Temple on the Sabbath was the one event that would force their hand and Jeshua would finally raise up an army against them and the Romans. At least that is what Judas hoped to see. He as much as admitted it to me tonight. He told me he was tired of waiting and watching to see when Jeshua would finally declare himself as the Messiah. He is sure the Pharisees fear that their control over the people might be in danger of slipping, and there is only one sure solution, the complete and total elimination of the threat to their power."

"Surely, the Pharisees do not mean to kill Jeshua!"

"If you had seen the soldiers of the Temple when they came to Gethsemane to arrest him tonight, you would not question that. There was a full platoon of them and another two in the street outside the Garden. You would have thought they were going to quell a riot, not arrest one unarmed man."

"Tell me what happened, John!"

"We were in the Garden waiting for Judas, as Jeshua had been told. Judas came with the soldiers, leading them to Jeshua's side. He embraced Jeshua and kissed him on the cheek. When Jeshua spoke to him, he stepped back and looked at Jeshua's face in horror. Only then, when Jeshua spoke and the torchlight showed his face clearly, did Judas realize what he had done. Jeshua looked at him with great compassion and quietly allowed the soldiers to tie his hands. Judas moved away, then suddenly turned and ran out of the Garden toward town. More disciples arrived and started to put up a fight for Jeshua's release. Peter even drew a sword and severed the ear of one of Caiphas' guards!"

"Oh, no! Were any of the disciples hurt?" I asked.

"No. Jeshua very calmly told the disciples to lay down their arms and leave quietly, then he picked up the ear of the soldier and placed it back, healing it completely. The soldiers were astonished and stepped back from him as though afraid to lay hands on him. But the one in command placed a hand on Jeshua's shoulder and forced him along down the street. He looked at me as he passed by..."

John's fragile control broke and he sobbed for a moment before regaining control.

"Please, you must come with me. We have to help Jeshua!"

"Magdalene? John? What is the matter? What has happened?"

Eena stood in the hall behind me.

"I heard the sound of weeping and John's voice. Where's Jeshua?"

I turned to her and held out my arms. She ran to me, her frightened look telling that she had heard the conversation.

"Jeshua's been arrested by the Temple guards. We are going to see what we can do about getting him released. Stay here until we return."

"No! Please don't leave me here. Whatever happens can not be as bad as what I will imagine sitting here alone not knowing. Please let me come with you."

I looked over her head at John. His emotions were held tightly in check and I saw I would get no assistance from him in this. I nodded and released her.

"Dress quickly, then. We have no time to spare. Mara, give John some wine while he waits."

Eena and I quickly dressed and rejoined John. His clothing was more presentable and he looked calmer.

"Did they say where they planned to take Jeshua?" I asked John.

"Yes, Caiphas ordered him brought before the Tribunal."

I was stunned.

"In the middle of the night? That's unheard of!" said Eena.

"What better time to take care of Jeshua when his supporters on the Sanhedrin are home in their beds snug and warm? Eena, run to the home of Joseph of Arimathea and alert him to what has happened. Do not let them send you away without seeing Joseph directly. Tell him that Jeshua's very life depends on his quick action. Can you do this?" I asked.

"I can, Magdalene, I will accompany Joseph to the court and meet you there." She hurried out into the night.

After instructing the servants to notify the disciples of Jeshua's whereabouts, John and I ran to the court of the Sanhedrin. We were not admitted, of course, but I was able to glean certain information from the servants as they warmed themselves by the fire while they waited for their masters within the court. What I learned chilled me to the core of my being.

I took John aside and told him of my discovery that Caiphas intended to push through a guilty verdict of Jeshua, a verdict of blasphemy that would permit his death by stoning. It was then that Joseph arrived and hurried into the court after assuring us he would do all he could to have Jeshua set free.

The next two hours passed agonizingly slowly. We learned that both Annas and Caiphas and then the entire council had questioned Jeshua. The arrival of Joseph thwarted the plans of Caiphas for a speedy resolution, for it was Joseph that reminded the council that under Roman law, only the Roman governor could order the death of a prisoner. After deliberation, it was decided that Jeshua should be sent to Pilate for trial.

Jeshua was led out of the court with his hands tied before him. Eena cried out his name and burst into tears when we saw that the soldiers had treated him most cruelly. They had fashioned a wreath of thorns and laid it on his brow where it cut his skin. His garments had been ripped and I could see the marks of a whip on his back. As he passed, Jeshua looked into my eyes and I heard his voice begging me to be strong for Eena's sake.

We followed behind the soldiers as they led him to the home of Pilate. As we walked quickly, trying to keep pace with the soldiers, Joseph told us to what had gone on in the council, how they questioned him about being the Messiah, the promised one.

"Jeshua said not a word they could focus on. They pressed him to admit that he believed he was the one promised of old, but Jeshua turned their words back upon them. 'You have said that I am he,' Jeshua told them. 'I have never spoken those words, I have admitted to being the son of the Father, as we all are sons of the Father, but never have I lifted myself above any, in thought or word, for we are all the children of the Father.'"

"They all argued for close to an hour while the soldiers amused themselves interrogating Jeshua. I had never before been ashamed of being a part of the Temple, but I am truly ashamed of these events."

Joseph's voice broke and he was silent for a moment.

"I learned another piece of information from one of the servants whom I have befriended. This servant was here earlier, before the soldiers arrived with Jeshua, and saw Judas Iscariot arrive to speak with Caiphas. He overheard Judas pleading with Caiphas to release Jeshua, saying that he had made a terrible mistake. Caiphas just laughed. He told Judas his plan had worked even better than expected. He knew he could never influence Jeshua, but with the threat destroyed, the pretend Messiah, as he called Jeshua, would have no real power to influence the people."

I was shocked at the name of the betrayer: Judas Iscariot! He had been a real help to Jeshua and me from the beginning, and had seemed to form a true affection for me, despite his closeness also to Jeshua's mother. But as I thought about it, following along behind my husband and the soldiers through the narrow streets to Pilate's, I began to see how that very closeness to Mary could have resulted in this whole situation. Her steadfast insistence that Jeshua, as the Messiah, proclaim his right as heir to the ancient Hebrew line descending from David, could be the motive for providing information to the Sanhedrin that would assure Jeshua's call to arms. The incident in the Temple on the Sabbath before Passover had greatly angered Caiphas and the rest of the Sanhedrin. The moneychangers and the merchants who sold the livestock to be sacrificed on the Temple altars all paid dearly from their profits for the privilege of setting up shop within the Temple walls. The receivers of those hefty fees were none other than the very Council who now held within their hands the life of the one man who had the power to influence the people upon whom they depended for their very opulent lifestyle.

My stomach knotted in fear. I could feel the subtle but

ruthless hand of Mary in this. She would stop at nothing to have Jeshua's rightful claim to the throne of David. Now she had gone too far. She had somehow persuaded Judas that only by the threat of destruction at the hands of the Sanhedrin, could Jeshua be assured of his rightful place someday as King of the Jews.

Chapter 18

We reached the home of Pilate and were forced to wait outside while he questioned the soldiers and then Jeshua. Joseph of Arimathea made his identity known to the centurion at the door and he was permitted to stand just inside where he could hear the proceedings. After about half an hour, he hurried back to Eena, John and me and told us of the quiet conversation that so frustrated Pilate and tried his patience and of Pilate's decision to send Jeshua to Herod.

"He knows, that as a citizen of Herod's province, Jeshua should be tried by him unless a crime against Rome has been committed. He has not been convinced that this is the case, though the Sanhedrin representative did his best to persuade Pilate otherwise. I saw the way he looked at Jeshua, Magdalene. He is painfully aware of his connection to you and your family. I think he is sending Jeshua to Herod to relinquish the necessity of deciding the case."

"I can understand him doing that. We have become very close to his first in command and have exchanged valuable information to the good of both sides. This is his way of acknowledging that relationship with us. I do not know whether I can be grateful for that or not. The thought of Jeshua standing before that despot of a king makes my blood run cold. He cannot hope to get a fair decision from Herod. My God, Joseph! That man had Jeshua's cousin, John, beheaded on the whim of a young girl in hopes he could seduce her! What hope does Jeshua have with a man like that?"

I leaned my head against Joseph's shoulder and gave in to the fear I had fought so hard since John's arrival at the house three long hours before. My tears fell freely as Joseph comforted me. The shock and horror of the night's events were beginning to be too much for me to bear.

"I know you are distraught, Magdalene", he said softly, "but you have Eena to think about, and there may yet be a way to turn this around. You must now rely on your wits and on the direction from the Father that you even now are receiving. Open your heart and your mind to that direction, Magdalene. You cannot dissolve into helpless tears like another woman might. You know too well the import of what we all do here. Trust that these events will work in our interest, and know that we depend on you to help keep us all going, no matter the outcome."

I raised my eyes to his and saw the sorrow and the compassion.

"You speak as though you have already seen the conclusion."

He nodded slightly, then lowered his eyes, as though he could no longer bear to look upon my sorrow.

"You see his death?" I asked softly.

Joseph looked at me, his eyes shining with unshed tears.

"What is death, Magdalene, but the return of the soul to Spirit from whence it came?"

"How can he die now, when the Spirit of the Christ resides within? Does not the Spirit of Sananda, who overshadows him, have the power to protect Jeshua and deliver him from this?"

"Magdalene, we have no way of knowing whether this is indeed part of the Divine plan of the Father for Jeshua, for Sananda, or for us all. We can only continue to be open to the guidance we receive and trust that all is as ordained by the Father."

"Magdalene!" Eena's voice came to me from across the courtyard. She and John hurried to where Joseph and I stood in the shadows. I dried my tears hurriedly and turned to face them.

"Magdalene, they are coming out. Do you think they are going to release him?"

"Eena, I think we would be very naive to think this would end so quickly and easily. I feel there are other forces at work here that we have only begun to detect."

The soldiers left the house with Jeshua in their midst. He looked tired and unsteady. As the group passed, I tried to catch his eye to send my love to him and my strength. As I focused on him, he seemed to stand a littler taller, walk a trifle steadier, and as I watched him pass, his eyes met mine.

For a split second, we seemed to be frozen in time. I was aware of those around me and my physical surroundings, but all I saw were his deep blue eyes and the sudden light that shown forth. I then heard his voice and that of Sananda, though I saw that he did not speak physically to me.

"Magdalene," he said gently. "You know what is to come. Your heart and soul have prepared for this moment. I now ask of you that which you do not wish to hear. I ask that you accept whatever the next hours bring with courage and with strength. I will need that strength, my love, I must submit to the decisions made by Divine Will and by us all before our entry into this time and place. We have consented to be the ones to anchor the energy of light and love into the planet. We must see it through to the end, my love. Will you now awake fully to that which we have agreed and assist Sananda and me to its completion?"

I could feel the tears stream down my face. Images of what was to come played in my mind's eye and I knew that I, too, had agreed to see it through to the very end. I drew the energy in through my crown as Jeshua taught me so very long ago and concentrating it in my heart, sent it to Jeshua, visualizing him receiving the energy pulling it into his heart.

"I am not about to let you do this alone," I replied in my mind. "We are together in this, my beloved husband, on all levels, in all ways. Nothing can separate us or destroy the love we have for one another, just as nothing can prevent us from accomplishing that for which we have come. My love is yours, now and forever."

"Always remember, Magdalene, I will never leave you, no matter what the appearance. Promise me you will remember this."

"I promise, Beloved. No matter what the appearance."

Jeshua looked away and followed the soldiers down the street. He never missed a step. Our communication had taken place out of the realm of time and space, but the words and images remained sharply with me, and I knew what I had to do in order to save the man I loved more than life itself.

"John! Come quickly!" I called him to my side as a plan formed.

I quickly explained what I needed and the reason. He looked stunned for a moment, then I saw the resolve harden in his eyes and he nodded, hurrying quickly away.

"Eena! Find James and tell him to meet me at Pilate's with a group of followers. I have a plan that may get Jeshua released."

"Right away, Magdalene. Are you sure that they will bring Jeshua back here?"

"I am sure of it. Herod will make no decision that will jeopardize his tenuous relationship with Rome. He will send Jeshua right back to Pilate for judgment."

"Magdalene's right, Eena. Herod is too fond of his easy lifestyle to endanger it by angering Pilate. Go quickly, then return to your mother's house until I send word. If this ends the way I fear it must, she should be there to see the result of her handiwork." Joseph's voice was hard and cold, but one could hardly blame him. We all knew how much Mary had pushed for a physical claim for the Messiah.

Eena gasped and looked at me, frightened for us all.

"Do not think of the possibilities, little sister. Think only of the need Jeshua has now for us all to do our parts. Go quickly and do as we have asked." I hugged her briefly and she hurried off into the night.

I turned to Joseph and reached out to him for support. He clasped my arm firmly and led me to a low wall where we sat to rest. He signaled one of Pilate's servants for a cup of water and made sure I drank my fill before quenching his own thirst.

Joseph cleared his throat and took my hand. My heart lurched within my chest. I was very sure that I did not want to hear the words to come.

"We must prepare for the worst, Magdalene, and make preparations for the unthinkable. I have a tomb recently completed that lies a short walk from the place of execution used by the Romans. I will instruct my servants to prepare it to receive Jeshua. I will make sure they place within the tomb all things that may be needed, food, water, clothing, and healing herbs and ointments. No matter what the outcome, you will be provided for, my dear. I have come to think of you as a daughter, Magdalene. Please allow me to assist you as I can."

"Thank you, Joseph. How can I refuse an offer so filled with love? We have grown quite fond of you, both Jeshua and I. I will gladly accept your offer of assistance. May I ask another favor of you?"

"Anything, Magdalene. You have only to ask."

"I want to be able to be as close to Jeshua as possible when they return. Can you somehow arrange for me to be admitted to wherever he will be taken?"

"I'll do what I can. Wait here for me while I see to it."

I watched him as he moved to the group of servants preparing the courtyard for the day's activities. He spoke with them at length and then returned finally to me, carrying a small loaf of bread and a cup of wine, both of which he handed me.

"Here," he said, "eat while I tell you what I have discovered."

I divided the bread in half and urged him to eat, which he did with hesitation. The bread tasted no better than the sawdust from the floor of Jeshua's workshop, but I knew that I must have nourishment, not only for myself, but also for the new life I carried within. I sipped the wine and listened as Joseph told me of the Roman court's procedures and traditions. These correlated with the information received from Pilate's lieutenant on his many visits to my father's library. A glimmer of hope began to burn within my breast. Perhaps the worst would be prevented. I prayed that God would allow it to be so.

Part of me felt that I should have followed Jeshua to

Herod's, but part of me knew that I needed some kind of rest in order to allow me to see this through to the end, whatever that end might be. I pushed the thought of Jeshua's impending death from my mind, while at the same time constructing alternate plans for that very real possibility. The strategist that my father encouraged came to the forefront, and after a lengthy discussion with Joseph, I felt that we had covered all possible outcomes and had contingency plans for each. Though my heart did not accept the thought of separation from Jeshua, my mind had dealt too long with the reality of life to be tricked into ignoring the probabilities of the situation.

Dawn was rapidly approaching and the roosters just beginning their welcome of the new day when word arrived that Jeshua and the soldiers had returned from Herod's palace. By this time, word had spread of Jeshua's arrest and the courtyard quickly filled with curious people anxious to see this man about whom so many had spoken. Was this indeed the same man who had wrecked the Temple just days before? Was this the one whom some believed was the Son of God, or was he an impostor, a man who cared only for power and glory? I stood in the corner of the courtyard and pulled my shawl up over my hair trying to remain hidden as long as possible. I had traveled nearly everywhere at Jeshua's side the past three years and knew it would be only a matter of time before someone recognized me as his wife and companion. The longer I remained unnoticed, the longer I could concentrate on helping him through the ordeal to come.

Soldiers began pushing people to the side, and the contingent of guards surrounding Jeshua led him through the crowd to the steps leading to the platform where Pilate would appear. I gasped and clutched at my heart when I saw him clearly for the first time. Apparently, the guards at Herod's palace had amused themselves by inventing new methods of causing pain without permanent damage. Several streams of blood ran down Jeshua's face from the wounds inflicted by the crown of thorns pushed cruelly into his head.

His wrists also were scraped and raw from the bindings and there were bruises on his arms and legs from the beatings he had endured. Still, he stood there calmly, with great dignity, as the crowd began to push closer, trying to see his face, asking questions, then shouting jeers and obscenities when he did not reply.

Pilate appeared and the crowd roared its approval. The morning sun peeked over the top of the wall and shone off the brightly polished armor of his personal guards. He regally strode across the platform and sat in the chair placed in the center where all could see. His lieutenant handed him a scroll, which he studied for a moment before rolling it slowly and returning to the lieutenant. He looked thoughtfully at Jeshua, studying him intently.

As though he felt his gaze, Jeshua raised his eyes and looked at Pilate. I could feel the energy flow between them, and at that moment, knew with certainty that the worst would happen. Pilate was merely playing his part in the drama in which we all acted. My heart ached with sorrow. All I could do was help lessen the effects of what would most surely come.

I stood in the shadow of the wall and directed healing energy and light to Jeshua as he and Sananda had taught me. So deeply focused was I, that I did not see James' approach, only recognizing his presence when he spoke to me.

"I am here, Magdalene. What could you have me do?" he asked.

"James, your zealot friends are here. I suspect they will try to obtain the release of Barrabas or other of their supporters who have been jailed by Pilate. I beg of you, please persuade them to ask instead for Jeshua's release. Please, James! He must be freed! You know what will happen to him if he is not released!"

I had grabbed hold of James's robe in the attempt to persuade him to listen to me. He pulled my hands from his clothing and looked at me with great loathing.

"Do you have any idea how difficult it has been for me for all these years living in the shadow of the Messiah, knowing that whatever I did or said was not good enough? I never measured up to the great Jeshua, the first born and heir to the throne of David. Did you know that my mother ignored my existence so much that she refused me her breast at my birth? She ignored my presence as much as my father would allow it. She even stood by once as I was fished out of the river where I would have drowned had not a ten-year-old servant girl heard the splash and jumped in to save me. I am sick to death of living in his shadow. He has been given everything good in this life and I have been given nothing. Even you, Magdalene, he got simply because he was besotted with you from childhood. What a lucky man to have a mother who worshipped him and a beautiful wife with whom to share his life. And what have I, Magdalene? What?"

I was speechless. These last few years he had never once given me cause to think that his life had been the unbearable burden that he now would have me believe. The story about Mary I believed because I had firsthand knowledge of her intense desire to see Jeshua recognized as the Messiah.

"I'm truly sorry if you feel you have been overlooked in favor of Jeshua, but now is not the time to discuss how this occurred. We must do all we can to free Jeshua and get out of Jerusalem. Please, James!"

"You don't understand yet, do you, Magdalene? With Jeshua out of the way and no longer here to teach the people, who will they turn to for guidance? Although Jeshua has indulged your whims and allowed you to teach in public, you are, after all, only a woman. No one will listen to you. Who will lead them? Peter? That coward even denied knowing Jeshua when asked about it last night. None of the others are as well educated or as powerful. I will be the one to whom they will turn to lead them from under the yoke of Roman rule and into the glorious future that has been promised to God's chosen people." James smiled.

I looked at him, stunned by what I had just heard.

"You don't have any intentions of helping Jeshua, do you?"

"Why should I? If he is the real Messiah, let God help him! Nobody has helped me deal with this lifetime. Let Jeshua deal with this on his own."

He turned and quickly disappeared into the crowd.

Suddenly, the crowd yelled again. "Crucify him!"

I had been so engrossed that I had totally missed the proceedings with Pilate. What had happened to make the crowd so vehement towards Jeshua? Then I noticed that the group of zealots was strategically placed in the crowd and were encouraging them to influence Pilate's decision.

I fought my way to the front of the crowd and found myself next to John ben Zebedee.

"Are you here to help Jeshua or to see James destroy him and everything he has worked for these long years?" I asked.

John looked at me and I could see the pain in his eyes.

"I cannot believe that I was so taken in by him, Magdalene. I thought we were trying to accomplish the same thing, but he never heard a word Jeshua said about the next world and the world of Spirit, did he?"

"He heard, John. He just had his own plan all along. We cannot let him succeed, John, Too much is at stake."

The crowd roared their approval and I looked up to see the soldiers strip Jeshua's cloak from him, baring his back. Again, the crowd roared.

I screamed Jeshua's name in horror and disbelief as he was tied to a post at the front of the platform, his hands and arms wrapped around it. He heard my voice and searched for my face in the crowd, found me, and focused his attention on me. I heard Sananda's voice in my mind.

"Now, Magdalene. Center your energies and focus all you can to Jeshua. He needs all the strength you can send him."

The sight and sounds of the crowd slowly faded from my consciousness as I centered my being and began pulling in and concentrating the light and the love of the Father, focusing all toward Jeshua with every part of my soul. I saw only the deepest blue of his eyes and again saw the light that seemed to shine forth. There was only him, though I vaguely heard the crowd and the sound of the whip as it snapped repeatedly against its target. I sent forth all the love I had for him, willed him to see it blaze forth in my eyes, willed him to feel nothing but my love for him. Again and again, the whip rose and fell. Again the crowd roared and counted each stripe as it was laid across Jeshua's back.

I was not conscious of the tears streaming down my face or the fingernails digging into the palms of my tightly clenched hands. I did not feel John slip his arm around me to steady me, nor did I know when my brother Lazarus arrived and stood beside me for support. My only focus continued to be Jeshua. Only toward the end did he flinch at the sound of the whip meeting his back.

At the last count of thirty-nine, he closed his eyes and rested his face against the post. Pilate ordered Jeshua cut loose from the post and he slumped to the ground. I, too, would have fallen had it not been for the presence of John and Lazarus by my side. Pilate rose from his chair and went to Jeshua. He bent low and spoke softly to Jeshua, then strode back to his chair. He stood thoughtfully for a moment, then seemed to have reached a decision and turned to the crowd. He held up his hand for silence, and the crowd quieted.

"I have read all the charges brought against this man and I can find no serious crimes against the state, certainly no crime against Rome for which he should be punished. If you wish to lock him away for his delusions, then do so and leave me out of it."

Pilate turned, but was stopped by the voice of Caiphas.

"Pilate, I beg your indulgence," he said, climbing the stairs to the platform. "This man may not appear to be the kind of criminal as, say Barrabas, but the sedition he preaches is the worst kind. He has consistently preached that all men have the innate power to be free of any kind of tyranny and have the power to live any way they choose, in freedom from any one, god or man or government. This teaching is treason against Rome and the Emperor and as such, is punishable by death."

Caiphas appealed to the crowd.

"Have any among you heard this man teach those words?" he asked.

"Yes! I have heard this! Death to the traitor of Rome!" shouted a voice from the back of the crowd. Others of the crowd picked up his words, and soon all were shouting for Jeshua's death.

I looked at Jeshua. He simply closed his eyes against the pain. I looked at Pilate. His eyes met mine and held them briefly, as though he begged me to understand.

Pilate made one last attempt to save Jeshua. He walked to the front of the platform and looked down at the crowd, signaled for silence, and again appealed to them.

"This man has done nothing wrong that I can determine. According to Passover tradition, you are given the choice of one political prisoner to be freed. I now give you the choice: Jeshua or the murderer Barrabas."

The crowd screamed out its choice.

"Barrabas!"

I sobbed in frustration and pain. How could they choose the release of Barrabas over Jeshua, who preached only the love of the Father for all mankind? I screamed for Jeshua, hoping he could hear me above the crowd. He opened his eyes and looked at me steadily, and then I knew. He had known this would happen. He had known for some time of Sananda's merging with him at the time of the baptism. He had been trying to prepare me for the eventuality of carrying on after his death. I couldn't bear the thought of going on without him. Surely, something could be done to prevent this. Suddenly, from deep within me, came a flooding forth of strength and determination. I was far from useless, even if I was a woman. There were options available to me that few others would even be aware of, and I would make sure that I did all in my power to save Jeshua's life.

I turned to John and gave him instructions to meet me at Golgatha in an hour. I told Lazarus to send for Eena and Mary. There was no way she was going to be spared from the sight of what her treachery had accomplished. Somehow, out of defeat, we would find triumph.

I gestured to Jeshua of my love and that I must leave. He nodded slightly and I understood that he was ready for what was to come. He had accepted the inevitable. I had not. As I pushed my way through the crowd to the gate of the courtyard, I heard Pilate ask the crowd what to do with Jeshua. The answer was deafening.

"Crucify him!"

Chapter 19

Those words echoed in my ears as I hurried to Golgatha, the hill of execution. Crosses dotted the hillside and the path leading to the crest of the hill. I saw the centurion on duty and recognized him as an old family friend. I motioned him away from his group, told him of the events that had transpired, and asked for his help. He readily agreed, and assured me that all would be as I requested.

I sat on a rock in the shade of a small tree while I waited for the rest to arrive. Three crosses had been prepared, so I knew there would be others who this day would also meet their deaths at the hand of the mighty Roman Empire. Yet, though my thoughts were of Jeshua's impending death, I was calm inside. I kept remembering Sananda's words to me earlier.

"I will never leave you, no matter what the appearance."

There was wisdom that I needed to hold tightly. I repeated those words as though they were a magical formula that would ensure a miracle. And maybe they would, I thought.

Too soon, I could hear the approach of the procession, and the crowd that invariably gathers to witness the bizarre ritual of crucifixion began to collect. The centurion had already seen to it that the barricades I requested were in place, and I took my place close to the area that had been set aside for the families of those who were to die. I heard someone call my name and saw Eena running towards me, crying piteously. She threw her arms around me and sobbed inconsolably. I held her close and tried to comfort her, but I was too near that point myself to be of much comfort. I could not tell her all would be well, for certainly, all was anything but well.

For three long years, all our waking moments had been devoted to the teaching of God's love to those with whom we connected. We told of the way each and every one is loved and gifted by the Father with abundance, freedom of choice, and the talents and abilities of choosing the way of Light and love over that of darkness and ignorance of God's love. We had dedicated our lives to the work we had come to do, and now, I waited to see the end of all that we had worked so hard to accomplish. Yet, in spite of knowing full well what was to come, I still trusted that all was part of the plan. I certainly could not see it, but I had to trust that the Father had a plan and a reason for all this.

The noise of the crowd suddenly picked up, and we knew that the condemned prisoners had arrived. My heart fell as I saw that Jeshua was being helped by one of the soldiers, and another carried the cross meant for him. Jeshua staggered unsteadily, even with the soldier assisting him. I put my hand out to touch Jeshua, as did Eena, and was pushed aside by the soldier to make way for the cross.

As Jeshua was laid down upon the crude wooden cross, I turned Eena from him and hid her face in my shoulder.

"Don't look, Eena, not now."

I held her tightly and watched as heavy spikes were driven into Jeshua's wrists to fix him to the crossbar. He was also tied with heavy ropes so his body weight would not pull the nails from his wrists. When his wrists had been nailed, his feet were fixed in place on the bottom bar with a single nail even larger than the first two. I tried very hard to be brave for Jeshua, but I could not watch them hammer the nails into those hands that only yesterday had lovingly caressed me. I could not watch the nail being driven into his feet, the feet that I had anointed with perfume and dried with my hair.

I closed my eyes again when they lifted the cross into place and heard and felt his agony as the cross bounced into the ground, tearing his flesh where the nails held him firm. After a moment, I found the courage to open my eyes and saw him watching me with such love and pity. It was as though he was asking my forgiveness for putting me through this ordeal. As soon as the soldiers had finished securing the cross and cleared the debris from the area, my father's centurion friend came to me followed by a young soldier carrying clean cloths, water, and a carafe of potent wine.

"Magdalene," he said, "you will need this for him. He will grow very thirsty when the sun reaches the zenith. The wine you must give him all day periodically. It will dull his senses and permit an easier death. When those you have sent for arrive, I will have them sent to you."

He leaned down and kissed the top of my head just as he had done all my life.

"I am so very sorry, my dear", he said. "Thank you for letting me be of service to you. And him. He is truly all they say of him, isn't he?"

I nodded and smiled, brushing the tears away.

"Yes, he is. All that and so much more."

Before he left, he led us to a place behind the barricade where we would be apart from the crowd and those who delighted in heckling the family and friends of the dying men. Eena and I sat on the ground and for the first time, she saw Jeshua's state. She burst into tears yet again, then quickly controlled herself.

"I can be strong for Jeshua, too, Magdalene, just like you. There will be plenty of time for tears later. How can I help him?" she asked.

"Find that calm place inside we talked about. Then see the energy of God flow into you through your crown and send it to Jeshua out through your heart, wrapped in all the love you have for him."

"I can do that," she said, and did.

We both sat there sending all the strength to Jeshua that we could. Sometime later, how long I could only guess, John arrived with bad news. The blowfish poison I had asked him for that would imitate the symptoms of death had been misplaced. His brothers were searching for it and would bring it when it was found. I was frantic at first with the news.

"If we give it to him too late, it will not work as it should. It may truly kill him rather than just give the appearance of death. They must find it, John, they must!"

"It will arrive in time, Magdalene. We cannot give it to him too soon, either. It must look as though his death was directly caused by the crucifixion. How is he bearing up?" John looked up at Jeshua, who had his eyes closed.

"He has been quiet, for the most part, trying to reserve his strength. He spoke a short time ago to those who are on either side. The one on the left mocked him, saying that if he truly were the Messiah, he would get down off the cross and save himself. The one on the right spoke up in Jeshua's defense saying that they deserved their fate, for their crimes against mankind. Jeshua, he said, had committed no wrongdoing and did not deserve to be crucified with them. Then he asked Jeshua to remember him to the Father, when Jeshua stood before him. Jeshua then told him they would today meet in Paradise. Oh, John, how can God allow Jeshua to die?"

My voice broke and I could not speak without losing the very fragile control I possessed. Now was not the time for helpless weeping. I feared that would come all too quickly. John put his arm around me for comfort. I was glad of his presence, for I knew I would need the support of his friendship.

"Where are the others of the twelve?" I asked. "Surely, they have all heard of Jeshua's plight."

"They are afraid, Magdalene. They also have families and their ties to Jeshua are too well known to risk being seen here with a condemned criminal. They are afraid of reprisals from the crowd and from the Sanhedrin. If this happened to Jeshua, the one we all believed was the Messiah, the Chosen One, what is to say they will not try to be rid of the rest of us as well? They have not heard all of Jeshua's words, have not pondered the enormity of what is done here. They can see only here and now, not the glory of the life in Spirit to which we will all return. They are simply men, Magdalene, afraid for their lives and those of their families."

"I understand, John. I have heard each and every word Jeshua has spoken, seen things that make me know the truth of those words, yet I, too, am fearful, fearful of life without him. But I know I must go on, no matter what happens, for his child that I carry within."

"I will help in any way I can Magdalene. You can depend on me."

"I know, John, and I am grateful for your friendship to both me and Jeshua."

I looked at Jeshua, so pale and still on the cross. The pain that he endured from the position in which he was placed made each and every breath a searing agony, yet he had refused the drugged wine given me by the centurion for him and would accept only sips of water offered him on water-soaked cloths. The first time he refused, I, myself, carried the cup to the foot of the cross, begging him to reconsider.

"Jeshua, please!" I begged. "Do not prolong the pain, my love. I cannot bear it. Please!"

I sank to my knees at the foot of the cross in tears. I set the cup against the rocks that supported the cross and embraced the rough wooden tree that held the ebbing life of the only man I would ever love. My fingers caressed the rough splintered wood as I longed to caress my husband, to comfort him and to lessen his pain. My fingers encountered wetness, and I saw that my hand was wet with his blood. I looked up at him and saw that he watched me.

Jeshua looked down at me with such love and compassion, and I felt the energy of his love reach out to me and embrace me.

"Magdalene, my love," I heard him say with my heart and mind. "Please do not cry so. The wine does not lessen the pain of having to leave you here. It only prolongs the agony of watching you suffer with me. Please take Eena and go now."

"I cannot leave you, Jeshua," I whispered. "Please do not ask me."

He closed his eyes then and nodded. I did not approach

the foot of the cross again. It was simply too painful for both of us.

I heard a commotion to my right and saw Jeshua's mother, Mary, accompanied by her cousin, also Mary, and Jeshua's brother, James. John stood at their approach and faced Mary, determined to make her see the result of her manipulations. She looked confused and bewildered, as though she was unsure of why she was there. I placed my hand on John's arm to silence him.

"Mary, have you come to see your son? Have you come to see Jeshua?" I asked.

"James said he was here, but I don't see him anywhere. Why have you tricked me into coming here?" Her eyes shown with hatred, recognizing me as I allowed the shawl to fall from my hair.

"Mary, there is your son," I said gently, and gestured toward the cross.

"No, that cannot be Jeshua. I have come to hear him declare himself the Messiah."

"Look carefully, Mother," said Eena, stepping forward. "There is Jeshua. There are the results of your political games. Jeshua now hangs from the cross dying. Are you proud of your plots now, Mother? How do you feel now?"

Eena reeled from the hard slap Mary gave her.

"You are no longer my mother. I will never forgive you for all of this."

Eena turned and ran to Lazarus and Bethel who had just arrived with Simon. Bethel opened her arms to Eena and comforted her as she wept bitter tears. Simon, also, placed his arm around her for support.

"Enough of this, James. Where is Jeshua and why have you brought me here?" Mary's voice was cold and hard.

"Magdalene is right, Mother." replied James. "It is Jeshua who is being executed for crimes he never committed, thanks to his betrayal by Judas, who led the soldiers of the Sanhedrin to him."

"He was to have declared himself to them and raised his followers to rout the Romans! Jeshua!" She turned to the cross and would have thrown herself at Jeshua's feet had not John caught her arms and stopped her.

"You will not make this any harder on Jeshua that it already is. You may speak with him, but there will be no display of histrionics. For once in your life, think of him first." John's voice was low and hard, for he did not wish Jeshua to hear.

Mary turned on John, spitting out her words with hatred and virulence.

"How dare you speak to me is such a way! My whole life has been centered around bearing the Messiah and seeing him ascend the throne of David, taking his place as the rightful heir. My only thoughts have been of him, my only desire that he surround himself with those worthy to be in the presence of the Messiah, the Chosen One. Instead of those versed in the ancient ways and traditions, he has drawn to him common people, fishermen, carpenters, tax collectors, and harlots. Even the one he made his bride is of dubious character, a whore from the Temple of Isis, a priestess who no doubt gave herself willingly to any man who sought communion with the heathen Goddess. I am the only one who has always had his best interest at heart, the only one who truly understood what he was to become, the one true King of the Jews!"

Mary turned to look at Jeshua and burst into tears.

"Now look at my son, the King of the Jews. It should not be my firstborn, not the Chosen One of God. All my hopes and dreams, all my plans for the future have come to naught. Oh, Jeshua, why could you not have listened to my words and taken them to heart. My son, my son!"

John helped her to sit on the ground and held her for a time letting her cry out her grief and disappointments. I could not reach out to her. There was a block of ice within my heart that blocked all pity for her. I had seen firsthand what her plans for Jeshua and her antipathy towards James had wrought. The final results were before us all and she could no longer deny her part in it.

"Magdalene," said John softly. "James stands apart and

would like to speak with you."

My first impulse was to ignore his request, but I realized that if any healing was to come from this tragedy, I would have to be open to the possibilities. As I walked to where he stood, alone and isolated, I could feel that he had always felt so. How difficult it must have been to grow up with his brother constantly held before him as the savior of the Jews, to be worshipped and adored and emulated. Was it any wonder he had chosen as he had? Would I, in his position, have chosen any differently?

James let his cloak fall to his shoulders as I approached and I saw he had cut his hair and was now clean-shaven. He was stepping out from the shadow of the older brother and had altered his appearance accordingly. As I studied him, I could see he had been weeping. I held out my arms to him and we held each other in a hard embrace. We had been through a lot together, he and I, and the love I felt for him as Jeshua's brother and my friend helped me to forgive the actions that had led to this end.

"Magdalene, can you ever forgive me? I must have been mad to have caused this. Jeshua is my brother and I have known for years that I am not on the same level as he. He truly is the one chosen as the Messiah. I have thought on his words to us all and I can see now that he never meant to take a physical throne. He spoke only of the world of Spirit and the life we share with the Father. I have been a fool, Magdalene. I, of all people, who was with him through the studies, who watched him with the learned teachers of every clime, listened as he dumbfounded the spiritual masters of every land, I above all, should have seen what he was about. I should have known and helped. Instead, I have destroyed it all, and him, in the process!"

He broke down and wept bitterly. John, who had heard every word, placed an arm around him, and embraced his friend. The two held each other sharing their grief and remorse. After a moment, James composed himself and turned to me.

"Magdalene, do you think Jeshua would let me tell him

how very sorry I am? I realize it won't change anything."

I took James' hand and led him to the cross.

"Do you not remember, James, the answer Jeshua gave to the man who asked how many times we should forgive? Jeshua said seventy time seven. Tell him what is in your heart."

When we reached the foot of the cross, we saw Mary and Jude standing there. We joined them silently, too filled with grief to speak. Jeshua looked down at us gathered there and smiled gently.

"Put this behind you," he said softly.

He then looked down into his mother's face with love and understanding and said, "Woman, behold your son."

Then he looked at James. "Son, behold your mother."

"Love one another as I have loved each of you," he said.

James touched his mother's shoulder tentatively, and for the first time in all the years I had known them, I witnessed Mary reaching out to him. He held her close for a moment and then led to her a space away where he, John, and Jude then sat together, waiting for the end.

Although the hour approached midday, the sky had darkened and it looked as though a storm was fast approaching. There was lightening on the horizon and the distant sound of thunder. Where were John's brothers with the blowfish? If they tarried any longer, the intended effects for Jeshua would be too late. Just then, the centurion's assistant came running to me.

"Pardon me, ma'am, but the centurion asks for your presence. There is one at the entrance who is asking for you and says his business with you is urgent. Will you come?"

"Yes, of course," I said, then called to John.

We received the poison from his brother at the gate and mixed it into the drugged wine. We hoped the timing would be all right. The poison had the power to cause the appearance of death, and if the antidote was administered within the allotted time, the effects would be counteracted and Jeshua restored to life. At least that was the plan.

Jeshua at first refused the wine. John then got permission to climb up the ladder and personally give it to him and in the pretext of helping him drink from the cup, explained the purpose of the wine and what we hoped to achieve. Jeshua drank deeply from the cup, and I breathed a sigh of relief. Now there was a chance we could save him. I also hoped that the wine would lessen his pain. His breathing became more shallow and forced due both to the position and the pain that breathing caused him.

As he suffered through the long hours, I tried to retain my composure for his sake. Those times that the pain and grief overwhelmed me, I turned away and hid my face from him to spare him the sight of my weeping. We did not speak more than a handful of words, for they were not necessary. We both knew what lived within our hearts and souls for one another and I clung to the words of Sananda and Jeshua earlier. "I will never leave you, no matter what the appearance."

As the storm approached, the sky darkened even more and a cold wind began to blow. In the dimmer light, I saw Jeshua's aura. The color was darker than I had ever seen and the grayness of it alerted me to the possibility of imminent death. I watched more closely for signs that the poison was taking effect and saw that his coloring had taken on a bluish tint and his breathing was so shallow as to be unnoticeable. Suddenly, a load clap of thunder startled us and I saw Jeshua open his eyes for the first time in over an hour.

Jeshua looked up at the gathering gloom and in that instant, I saw a light that seemed to rise from Jeshua and disappear. His body stiffened and he cried in a loud voice.

"My God, My God! Why have you forsaken me?"

I looked up, stunned by what I had seen. The spirit of Sananda had departed from Jeshua.

"No!" I screamed. "No, don't do this!"

I knew at that point that Jeshua was within moments of death. The centurion approached and told me in a low voice that the guards were approaching to break the legs of those on the cross to speed their deaths. He said that since Jeshua was obviously so near death, he could stop them by piercing his side with a spear.

"Magdalene, he is suffocating. If I do this now, he may still survive."

I nodded my approval.

Before the centurion had returned with his spear, Jeshua again lifted his head. He looked briefly into my eyes and I knew the moment had come. The poison had arrived too late; the spear would be too late. Jeshua was dying before my eyes and I could do nothing to prevent it.

He looked at the sky, took a deep breath, and said, "It is finished."

His head dropped to his chest and I knew I had lost him. I ran to the foot of the cross and collapsed weeping. John came to my side, but I would not be consoled. My only reason for existence had left this life and I could see no reason to go on. I had no rational thoughts and no focus. John pulled me away from the cross to allow the centurion to pierce Jeshua's side, which caused me to weep even more.

The centurion came to me and said softly to me in the guise of condolence, "He yet lives. Do not give up hope just yet."

I kept my face hidden so my sudden joy would not be apparent to those around me. He lived! There was hope! We had to get him down quickly and to a place where he could be tended. I called for John and had him send word to Joseph of Arimathea that the time had come. Joseph had not waited for my word, however, and had already received permission from Pilate to have Jeshua removed from the cross as soon as death had been determined and gave him permission to inter the body.

The antidote had to be administered within an hour of the appearance of death in order to restore life to the body. Time was passing too swiftly now. The antidote could not be administered until Jeshua had been removed from the cross and taken to the tomb that now awaited him. The family waited for Joseph to arrive with Pilate's permission to remove the body. Nothing could be done until then.

Finally, the servant presented the papers to the centurion

and the task of removing Jeshua without doing further damage to his body began. Mary and the other family members present were now loudly wailing and mourning, as was the custom. I understood, and wanted to be able to let go and join them, but knew I could not. Too much was at stake. I watched impatiently as James, John, and Lazarus carefully and gently removed Jeshua from the cross, tearing his flesh from the nails. I comforted myself with the thought that at least he could not feel the pain now.

They passed Jeshua down and I held out my arms for him. They laid his head in my lap and covered him with my cloak. I checked carefully for signs of life, and sure enough, I could detect a faint pulse in his throat and the shallowest of breaths. John ran for the wagon and I sat rocking him in my arms, crying and begging him not to leave me, pleading with him to hold on to the thin strand of life just a while longer.

Suddenly, his body convulsed and he gasped and stopped breathing.

Jeshua was truly dead.

"No!" I cried. "No, you cannot leave me! You promised you would never leave me!" and I sobbed uncontrollably, rocking him back and forth.

I was aware of people standing in front of me. I looked up to see Mary, James, and Jude staring down at me. Jude and James looked bereft, but Mary's look was pure hatred and disgust.

"You whore!" she shouted at me. "You priestess whore! This is all your fault! Jeshua's death is all your fault!"

She spat on me and would have struck me had not Jude and James physically restrained her and took her away. I sat there stunned at her words and the venomous tone of voice. She believed I had caused Jeshua's death.

The skies opened and the rains began. I sheltered Jeshua's body from the rain and waited for the wagon to arrive. My husband lay dead in my arms. It seemed not strange at all that the very heavens would mourn along with me.

* * * * *

Writing of that horrible time was very difficult for me. I felt anew the pain that Jeshua had endured and the despair and hopelessness that settled in my heart. I recalled the feeling of Jeshua's blood as it dripped onto my hand and the feel of the rough, splintery wood beneath my fingers and knew that I had not imagined it all. These memories were what I had recorded and what now must be written down. Although the crucifixion was excruciatingly and emotionally hard to recall, I know there is a higher purpose in my feeling the burning need to record the events of my time with Jeshua and to make it available for others to read.

All was not to remain in darkness, however, for after the darkest night of the soul comes the light and the promise of a new beginning, of hope for the future. I knew that I had survived the absolute worst that I could see and recall. The next event was to be the catalyst that set in place the establishment of the organized Christian church and the spread of Jeshua's words throughout the world. As Jeshua's death was part of God's divine plan, so was his resurrection.

Chapter 20

I walked beside the wagon in the rain, my heart and soul numbed by the day's events. Only the support of Joseph's arm around me kept me from falling. I held tightly to the side of the wagon as I stumbled over the uneven ground from Golgatha to the garden in which Joseph's tomb was located. He had reassured me several times of its close proximity, but each step seemed to drag longer than the one before. My life had ended an hour past with Jeshua's when he died in my arms. I could still feel his warmth slip away, still hear his mother's shouts of derision in my ears, still see the look of hatred for me on her face.

The wagon suddenly stopped. I was thrown off balance and would have fallen had it not been for Joseph's steadying hand. We had arrived at the tomb. My heart rebelled against the very thought of putting Jeshua to rest in that cold, dark place. My mind had shut down in grief. I moved without conscious thought where Joseph directed me.

Joseph, his servant, and John ben Zebedee carried Jeshua from the wagon into the tomb and laid him on the bedding that had been prepared for him. Joseph dismissed the servant and told him to stand guard at the entrance. I looked at him, questioning the order.

"If we are to succeed in bringing him back, we must not be disturbed," Joseph said in answer to my silent question,

"Do you think there is still time?" asked John. "Is it not too late to give him the antidote?"

"No one but God knows the time for death. I do not feel the time has yet come for Jeshua to depart this plane of existence. As he brought back the soul of Lazarus, Magdalene's brother, from the next plane, so will we, with the Father's grace and blessings, go forth to bring the soul of

Jeshua back to its physical form. Magdalene, will you and John wash and anoint him and bandage his wounds while I prepare the antidote?"

John and I worked together, gently washing the dried blood and caked dirt from Jeshua's body. I retained my composure until we turned him over to attend to his back. I gasped when I saw the extent of the damage done to his back by the whip, the skin laid open and ripped away in places. My stomach rolled and I ran out the door retching and sobbing.

When my stomach was empty and my tears subsided, John brought me a damp cloth. He gently wiped my face and offered me a drink of water.

"Sit here in the fresh air for a moment, Magdalene, while Joseph and I finish. We are nearly ready to administer the antidote."

I sat obediently on a rock at the door to the tomb. I could hear their quiet words as they discussed which ointments to use on Jeshua's wounds. I tried to center myself, tried desperately to reach out to Jeshua's soul, to Sananda, to anyone who could help. But I was filled with a penetrating cold and numbness. I could not even remember how to pray. No matter how I thought I had prepared myself for the possibility of Jeshua's death, nothing came close to the reality. In a few short hours, my purpose for living had been wrenched from me. If my heart had been ripped from my chest still beating, I would have been in no more pain than now. If there was a hell, then surely, this must be it.

Darkness was falling fast. Though the rain had stopped, the wind still blew cold and I started shivering. Still, I hesitated to reenter the tomb, to face the physical reality that awaited me.

Joseph spoke quietly to me.

"Come, Magdalene; it is time."

We entered the tomb and the servant rolled the stone to partially close the entrance, concealing it with brush to hide the dim lights of the two small lamps inside that had been lit. He then built a fire that would further conceal the tomb's joined us in our quest for the return of Jeshua's soul to the physical was so intense that I shivered with the strength of it, feeling it move through my body, causing the hair on the back of my neck and scalp to stand on end.

I looked across the body of my husband at Sananda. He nodded slightly, indicating that he also waited for my direction. I raised my hands in supplication, palms up. The others followed my lead. I closed my eyes and spoke from my heart, asking the mercy of the Father and the compassion of the Mother. I emptied my heart before the Father, on the altar of my husband's body, asking only that Divine will be manifest, surrendering all to the Father, affirming "not my will, but thine be done", and truly meant every word, for I knew within that I would survive Jeshua's absence. Friends and family would look after my child and me. But the greater purpose of what Jeshua had taught and done would be lost for all time unless there was in some way a miracle so undeniable that the words and teachings would be kept alive through the telling of the event. Jeshua's return from the dead would be such a miracle.

I have no clear memories of the words I said or anything I did, other than place my hands on Jeshua as I was led to do by whatever hand of Spirit assisted me through the long night. I recall little other than the flow of energy through my body to Jeshua's through my hands, the knowledge that all within the tomb, whether in Spirit or physical also accessed the same energy with the express purpose of healing Jeshua's body, and the realization that my surrender to the will of God in this matter was total.

I do not know how long we knelt in prayer and supplication. At some point in the long hours that followed, we took sustenance, drinking the cool water from the jug and eating bits of the bread from the loaf. I reapplied the healing ointments to Jeshua's wounds and gently wiped his face with a damp cloth. As I rubbed the ointment into the wounds on his feet, I recalled drying his feet with my hair the day of his return to Bethany. We all continued through the night, through the dawn, and into the next day doing what we could to heal Jeshua, calling his soul back from the etheric planes, never giving up or doubting that the will of God would prevail.

Always at least three of us worked on Jeshua leaving his side only briefly through the day. When the sun set on the second day, Joseph mentioned quietly that a group of followers had gathered outside beyond the soldier's camp and were praying and waiting for word. Somehow they had learned of our efforts and were keeping vigil with us, sending us love and energy. The knowledge that others knew of our efforts and worked with us strengthened our resolve and intent. We deepened our meditative state and intensified the flow of healing energy to Jeshua. Early in the morning of the third day, just before the cock's crow, Sananda spoke to me, bringing my consciousness back from the inner planes.

"Now is the time, Magdalene. Now you must call him back to us."

I looked at Sananda through the tears that formed. I knew that if our effort did not succeed now, Jeshua would be lost to us and must remain in spirit.

I again closed my eyes and visualized Jeshua standing before the Father. I recalled the words he had spoken to call Lazarus back to the physical world and spoke them clearly out loud.

"Father, I thank you for hearing me. I know you hear always when we ask for your blessings. I ask not for myself, but for those who will hear of what occurs here today, that they may truly know of the power of thy will and the love that is manifest for all your children. So they may also know that it is indeed you that has sent Jeshua into the world to show this love and light to all."

I took a deep breath and called to me all the power, love, and pure intent within me. Then in a clear and commanding voice I called: "Jeshua! Come forth! Return to us here and now, that the will of the Father may be seen and his mercy known to all. Jeshua! Return!"

The energy grew around us and suddenly the ground shook and a brilliant, almost blinding light filled the tomb. I felt a sudden heat, the touch of Lord Michael's hands on my shoulders and a peace in my heart so strong that tears began to fall.

I did not open my eyes, but clung to the deep belief that it was the will of God that Jeshua return to us. I sat patiently with my hands resting lightly on Jeshua's feet. A few moments later, Joseph whispered, "Look!"

I felt a slight tremor, a movement beneath my hands, and opened my eyes as Jeshua gasped for breath. He breathed deeply several times and then his eyelids fluttered. I moved quickly to his side and wiped his face with a damp cloth, noticing the color returning rapidly to his face. He raised his hand weakly. I grasped it tightly and held it to my heart. He asked for water and took a small sip from the cup that John offered him. His hand tightened around mine and he opened his eyes. Looking at me, he smiled a small tentative smile.

"Welcome back, Jeshua. How do you feel?" asked Joseph.

"As though I have been lying on the ground too long," he replied with a smile. He tried to move slightly and winced with pain. "I still have some healing to do. How soon can we get out of here?"

Joseph took command of the departure, arranging for the wagon's return and a distraction to draw the guards from the entrance.

* * * * *

For the next forty days, Jeshua rested and healed. We took him to Mount Carmel and asked the Essenes, who were gifted healers, to assist in his recovery. During the first two weeks, the spirit of Sananda continued to take on physical form and he appeared suddenly to many who had been followers of Jeshua. I had alerted the twelve to the fact of Jeshua’s resurrection but did not tell them of his location, only that he would see them as necessary. When Sananda appeared to them, they assumed that it was Jeshua and both Jeshua and Sananda thought it best. If it had been widely known that Jeshua had physically recovered, those who had plotted his death to begin with might be tempted to arrange a repeat.

Chapter 21

We stayed very quiet during the time of Jeshua's recovery, which was very rapid considering the extent of bodily damage he had suffered. As soon as Jeshua was strong enough and very close to the end of the forty days, Sananda again merged with Jeshua. I was delighted and relieved to have my twin flame and my beloved husband again in one, but it was not to last.

It had been an absolutely glorious day, the first one since the Crucifixion that I felt as though things might turn out all right in spite of the problems. We all gathered at Lazarus and Bethel's house for dinner. The disciples arrived in small groups from the various areas in which they had been traveling. The noise level increased steadily with each new arrival. Added to that was the sound of Lazarus and Bethel's six children and the children of the group as they romped and squealed and chased each other around the yard. Jeshua had as much fun as the children, chasing them with a growl, then turning and running in mock terror. As I watched smiling, I hugged myself in delight, placing a hand on my flat belly that even now held the tiny beginnings of a new life. Jeshua left the children, despite their protest at the loss of their playmate, and dropped to the ground beside me. He took my hand and pulled me down to sit in his lap.

"How are you feeling, Magdalene? Have you had any more sickness?" he asked.

"No, Jeshua, none since I woke this morning. It's nothing but an annoyance. It will soon pass. At least that's what Bethel says. She's had six babies, she should know." I snuggled closer and put my arms around his waist. "It won't be long until I'll be too heavy so sit on your lap."

Jeshua held me tight for a moment and kissed my forehead. The sun was beginning to go down. The breeze was cooler now, and I shivered. Jeshua helped me to my feet and stood.

"Run in the house and get our cloaks, would you? I don't want you getting a chill in the evening air."

"Won't we be going into supper soon, Jeshua?"

"Not for a while, dearest. I want to see the moon rise and the stars come out one last time."

My heart fell and my world stopped cold.

I looked into Jeshua's eyes and saw pain and regret.

"What do you mean, the last time?" I demanded. My heart beat wildly. The fear of his answer threatened to overwhelm me.

"What we merged together to accomplish has been fulfilled. Tonight Sananda will return to Spirit."

"No! You can't leave the baby and me! What about the baby?" I gripped Jeshua's arms with all my strength.

He pulled me to him and held me close. I was too full of fear and pain to even cry.

"Beloved!"

I could feel the pain of Sananda in his voice, the way he trembled as he held me tighter still.

"Beloved, surely you do not think that I would choose to depart now if there were any alternative. Jeshua and I have helped anchor the Christ energy. There are things I can attend to more readily from Spirit than in the physical. You will still have Jeshua's love and devotion, and I know you love him dearly. And I will be with you in Spirit, my dearest. I will never leave your side. Now, go get our cloaks. Please. I don't want you to get chilled."

He kissed the top of my head and looked down at me. I could feel his pain and sorrow at leaving me and knew that how I reacted would determine the tone of the evening for everyone else. So I took a deep breath and smiled. Granted, it was a small sickly smile, but it was a smile, nonetheless.

"I'll be right back." I kissed his cheek and turned away before my tears fell. I walked into the house not seeing the children in the yard, not hearing their playful shrieks and cries of joy. I walked past our friends and family members as though sleep walking. I went up to our room, the same room we had occupied as newlyweds, the same room in which I had first become aware of Sananda's presence. I shut the door and sat on the bed, trembling with the effort of staying in control of my emotions, but the memories flooded in and overwhelmed me. The first moments in Sananda's arms after the baptism, the return of Jeshua and our night in the garden. All the events leading to Jeshua's crucifixion and death, the travels and teachings, the strain between Jeshua and me because of his mother's plots, and the restoration of our relationship after what was being called the resurrection.. The last three years passed before me, the good and the bad, the joy and the despair. Suddenly, it was more than I could bear. I threw myself down on the bed and sobbed uncontrollably. I allowed the pain and despair to surface and gave vent to all the emotions I had tried so hard to suppress.

I had feared the coming moment every day since Jeshua's ordeal. I had known that Sananda's leaving was inevitable, as sure as the sunset that grew closer each minute. But now that the moment was at hand, I wondered how I would survive his loss. I knew logically that Sananda's presence would not leave my side, but I would no longer have him in the physical. My heart was breaking, tearing in half with the pain. Through the mist of pain that surrounded me. I was vaguely aware of the door opening and closing. Then strong arms lifted me, held me close and Sananda's voice slowly broke through the fog to my consciousness.

"Hush, Magdalene. It's all right dearest. I'm here. Don't cry, Beloved. Please don't cry. Don't you know how hard this is for me? Please, please, you'll make yourself ill if you don't stop."

He kissed me and caressed me and finally my sobs ceased. He gently wiped my tears and stroked my hair.

"We still have some time, Beloved, "he whispered softly. "I want this time with you alone."

Our lips met, and we lost ourselves in each other for a time, clinging desperately together one final time.

We left the house just as the sun set below the horizon and hand in hand slowly climbed the hill in the deepening dusk to join the twelve and those closest who knew of Sananda's presence. They were waiting for us at the top of the hill. The last rays of the setting sun caught Sananda as he stood on the crest of the hill and seemed to illuminate him in glowing light.

"Remember me," he said quietly to us all. "Recall why we were brought together here by the Father. To share the Light, to spread the good news of God's Love for all men and women, to show by example how to live in that Light and Love. You will all go from this place in time and will share the teachings of the Father with all those who hunger for Truth. And there are many who will hear your words and know of the Truth and awaken to their true identity as Children of the Father."

He made his way around the circle of loved ones that had formed before him and embraced each in turn, saying farewell with a smile, sharing a joke that brought laughter, a fond remembrance that brought a tear. The sun was completely gone now, yet the glow remained around him. When he had spent a moment with all save me, he looked at the moon rising over the crest of the next hill and silently held out his hand to me.

I placed my hand in his and we drew a few steps apart from the others. He stood with his arms around me gazing at the full moon and the countless stars.

"Ah, Magdalene. How I will miss this place and the warmth of you next to me. I know once in Spirit again I will not feel this illusion of separation, but now, my Beloved, I am suffering all the pain and despair of being human. This is the hardest thing I have ever had to do."

He turned and looked deeply into my eyes, holding my gaze.

"I promised you the day of my arrival that I would never leave you. Although I now must leave Jeshua, I will keep my promise to you. I will be at your side constantly, beloved, watching, protecting, guiding you and above all, loving you."

Then he looked again at the group gathered to bid him farewell, some of them weeping openly.

"Love one another as I have loved you. Remember to live as examples of God's love and light."

Sananda then turned to me and looked into my eyes.

"I will never leave you, Beloved. Lo, I am with you always, even until the end of the ages. Throughout eternity we have traveled, since our emergence from the Father when the morning stars sang together and the solar winds first blew. Together we will always be, until the evening stars burn out and all are returned to the arms of the Father. Never will I leave you, my beloved Magdalene. Never. Say that you believe this."

I couldn't speak, for the tears threatened and I did not want his last human sight of me to be one of tears and sorrow. I nodded and raised my hand to touch his cheek.

"I love you, Magdalene. Now and forever."

He stepped away from me and opened his arms wide, palms up. The glowing white light intensified and brightened and separated from Jeshua, rising above him into the night sky. We all watched as the soul essence of Sananda ascended till the glow of his light disappeared into the stars.

Jeshua swayed and John and I managed to catch him as he crumpled to the ground. He lay unconscious for several long moments. I cradled his head in my lap and John covered him with the cloak to shield him from the cold. When at last he opened his eyes, he appeared to be disoriented.

"Jeshua, are you all right?" I asked.

He looked up at me with such pain in his eyes. I knew that he was feeling the agony of separation as much as I. He reached for my hand and gripped it tightly. In the dim light I could see his eyes fill with tears.

"Magdalene, please," he whispered.

I looked up at the circle that surrounded us.

"Please," I asked, "can you leave us alone for a while? We'll come down later." I looked imploringly at John and my brother. "Please, Lazarus, can you show them to the house? I'm sure Bethel must be ready to serve dinner."

Lazarus took over and directed the group down the hill to where the servants were waiting with torches to light the way.

I could feel Jeshua's shoulders shake with the sobs that he had refused to allow in front of the others. I held him close, rocking him as we grieved our loss of Sananda. We sat there until the moon was at its zenith. When we had exhausted our tears, we shared our memories of the good times and bad and rejoiced in the knowledge that the child I carried was conceived of both Jeshua and Sananda, the perfect merging of our three souls.

By the time we returned to the house, the guests had departed and the household was in bed. Only Lazarus waited for us with cups of warmed wine to help banish the chill of the evening. We sat together in front of the fire drinking wine lost in our memories. Finally Jeshua stood and wearily made his way to the door.

"Thank you for the wine, Lazarus. Again your kindness touches me."

Lazarus rose and embraced Jeshua.

"You have been as my brother for all our lives, but even if there were no closeness between us before, the love and devotion you have for Magdalene would open my heart to you. I am doubly blessed to be able to call you brother in Truth. I, too, grieve Sananda's departure. The Father truly blessed us all with his Light and presence."

Jeshua nodded.

"Now," Lazarus continued, "there is but you to guide and lead us. You, alone, are left to continue the teaching in the world. Know that whatever I can do to assist in this, I will do. I will support you and Magdalene in any way I can. We will speak of this more tomorrow. You and Magdalene need rest now."

Jeshua clasped Lazarus' arm.

"I thank you, my old friend. Time enough for planning tomorrow. Goodnight."

He turned to me. "Are you coming, Magdalene?"

"I'll be there in a moment. I'd like to speak to Lazarus

first," I answered.

Jeshua smiled, but I could see how very weary he was. I longed to go to him, but I knew that this would be my only chance to speak privately with Lazarus. I watched Jeshua slowly climb the stairs, then turned to my brother. He stood beside the fireplace warming his hands. When he looked up and saw me, he said nothing, merely opened his arms to me.

When his arms enfolded me, all the heartache and pain of the day came flooding back and I dissolved in tears yet again. How safe and comforting it was to be held and nurtured by my brother! I was free to grieve only for myself, to allow the agony I felt within my soul at the separation from Sananda to surface. I indulged in feeling sorry for myself for a short time, then took a deep breath and dried my tears.

"Feeling better, or are you only tired of crying?" my brother inquired, we sat together then in front of the fire, his arms around me, my head resting on his shoulder. We sat often like this as children when I woke in the night crying for my mother. It felt good to lean on him again for support. "I'm better. Thank you."

"How's Jeshua handling all this?” Lazarus asked.

"It was a shock to him. I don't think he had any idea how very hard the separation would be on him. Having Jeshua will make it easier for me to bear, and I hope that I will be able to help him as well."

"Then go to him. It's late, and you both have been through a lot today." Lazarus embraced me and kissed the top of my head as he used to do when I was a child.

When I reached our room, I saw that the bed was empty. Jeshua stood by the window illuminated by the light of the full moon. His face was drawn and weary and he reminded me of a lost little boy.

I wrapped my arms around his waist and held him close. He was still cold to the touch.

"Why are you standing here? You should be in bed," I said.

"I couldn't go to bed without you. Oh, Magdalene, I feel

so very alone! I had no idea that Sananda's departure would be so difficult for me." Jeshua held me tightly, seeking comfort in my embrace as I sought mine in his.

"You are not alone, my love," I said. "I am with you every moment of every day. We have each other to help us through this time. And we have our child, the child conceived by the three of us in love. We have not lost Sananda, for he lives within our child and us. And knowing his sense of humor, I imagine we will hear his voice when we least expect it."

"I'm sure you're right, Magdalene. I am so glad you are here with me. I love you so very much and I regret deeply the discord between us. I should have listened to you and not my mother. I will not ignore your words again."

"We've put that behind us. Jeshua, I have loved you all my life. Nothing will ever stand between us again. I will not allow it."

"Neither will I. You are my rock, Magdalene. I depend on you for so much."

"As I depend on you, my love, That is the strength of our marriage, that and our love for each other. Now come to bed. We are both sad and weary and you are still cold. Come, let me warm you."

Jeshua held my face between his hands and looked deeply into my eyes. I saw the lines in his face soften in the moonlight and his eyes darken. He kissed me gently, then smiled.

"Yes, dearest, I need your warmth especially tonight." He swept me up in his arms and pulling the blanket aside laid me down in the center of the bed. He lay next to me, pulled the covers over us both and held me tightly to him. In no time at all, we were warm and fell asleep in each other's arms.

Chapter 22

In collecting the many channeled writings I have done with my guides and the notes concerning the regressions, I have generated many, many questions about the life in Palestine and the purpose of why we were there and what we hoped to accomplish. I also questioned why I was the one to write the book instead of another. As usual, Archangel Michael's channeled words cleared that up along with the burning question: did we know what was to come as far as the crucifixion and if so, why did we permit it to happen?

Michael

It was decided that one of the inner circle would be the one to recall the real details and to set the record straight. No one else had the perspective that the Master's wife enjoyed. Magdalene was privy to the real man more then all the rest of the entourage who were with him night and day. The final year before the crucifixion Jeshua became physically tired and emotionally depressed and unsure as to the continued worth of the mission. He knew the followers, even the inner group of twelve, were not understanding the complexity of what they were hearing, not understanding the simplicity of the required actions and changes needed for "salvation". Though he and Sananda spoke of the spiritual and the truth beyond physical life, the followers saw only the complications for life in the body. It was quite frustrating for both of them.

Jeshua's depression caused one of those "and he went into the wilderness for prayer and meditation" treks. The story of the temptation was really the story of Jeshua feeling very defeated and being uplifted by the angels and guides. The concerns and doubts he had were normal for the situation. He wanted some kind of proof that his words would be remembered by somebody. He was taken astrally to the Other Side and to the Hall of Records where he was shown the extent of the teachings' effect on the planet. He was also shown the crucifixion. The decision to continue or to abort the mission was left to him with the promise of no recrimination should his desire be to abort. The continuation of life after the crucifixion was given as an option and he was able to make the decision to carry on, even knowing of the end to which he might come. Although he was given the option of retaining life, the human body's frail condition made the option iffy at best. Sananda did not influence him, as far as persuasion goes, during this time, for the decision had to be Jeshua's alone. It is quite a thing to face death, but to see the details and know the extent of the physical abuse the body will undergo is something not many souls can cope with.

You ask why the task of the writing this book falls to you. The adoration and worship of Jesus and Mary, the mother, makes it impossible for those souls to incarnate and accomplish the reality check in regard to this. Magdalene is the only one who has not been elevated to "deity" and who could step forth and deliver the message as it was intended in the first place. Yes, many people are saying the same things. Many are recalling their lives with Jeshua and know they are remembering for a reason, but none of them have the memories that you do. No one has recalled the crucifixion with the emotion and heart wrenching detail that you did. No one has put the human touches on the man and his days of life. No one has spoken of the mystical and metaphysical aspects of the teachings and the happenings of those times.

We know the pain and anguish this whole thing causes you. We see the colors of your aura and heart chakra darken whenever you consider that time. We have seen the joy again in your heart as you relived the marriage to Jeshua, the early days of love between you, and the arrival of Sananda. We stood beside you and watched you fall apart as you recalled the crucifixion, the Resurrection, and the ascension of Sananda to spirit. Yet you realize that you will not fully put your lifetime in Palestine behind you until you have dealt with it totally and seen it all, the glorious times and the tragedies. This book is written from the heart and soul of the one who loved Jeshua and Sananda more than any other and the one who, in turn, is much beloved of them. It is your task to illustrate the humanness of the man and to stress that his mission was to teach that all can approach the Creators, Mother and Father God, directly, without a go-between.

Chapter 23

When we left Jerusalem, Jeshua and I split up to avoid detection. He traveled north and west with a small group catching a caravan headed to Gaul. They traveled much more slowly than we did. Joseph of Arimathea escorted Eena, Mary, and me, along with Simon and several others of the group, by caravan to Tyre. We traveled secretly hidden in wagons of goods bound for the port and far away markets. We all left within two weeks of Sananda's leaving us. By the time we reached Alexandria I was nearly four months pregnant but only Eena knew for sure. The others of the party were made aware of the fact during the next few weeks as my size expanded with that of the child.

Alta, the High Priestess in the Temple of Isis where I had been schooled for a time, received us in Alexandria and helped us in planning our journey. We knew of a community in Gaul that was partially Essene in origin but was less rigid in terms of diet and such. Alta used the scrying bowl in the temple to scry for us and described the community. She contacted one of them, a woman who had trained in the temple, telepathically and told of our coming. We followed that contact with a messenger sent by fast ship and one of our group who had been provided with enough money to purchase a residence with furniture and supplies. Alta provided much for us. By this time, Joseph's arrangements were completed and he had gathered plenty of funds and was well prepared for the journey. We chartered a ship rather than book passage so there would be no witnesses to our ultimate departure.

A few weeks later, I stood at the rail enveloped in a feeling of safety and protection by the small group of people surrounding me. I was on a ship in a river looking towards a landing of stone. It had been an important site in the past but now was unused. I was surprised at how desolate and abandoned it was. Whatever settlement or town had warranted the elaborate landing stage had totally disappeared. There were no buildings or foundations visible as we pulled up to the shore. I was also disappointed that we were not met for we should have been expected. There were green rolling hills and mountains in the near distance. After a time, we gathered all the belongings that we could carry and began walking. It felt good to walk after being cooped up in the ship for so long.

After a half day's walk we arrived at the outskirts of a small community where people came to meet us and apologized for not being at the landing to greet us when we arrived. Apparently, the timing of our arrival was off, either delayed or earlier than expected. They took us to a rather large house to rest and provided food and drink. I was grateful for the rest. I was eight months pregnant.

Within two days of our arrival our house was made available to us. It was smaller and cozier than we had lived in but I was greatly pleased just to have a place to lay my weary head. The village and the surrounding community treated us with great respect and deference. I was still considered a priestess of the Goddess and Jeshua's teachings and stories had reached even the ears of those in this place.

My daughter was born with Eena in attendance. Jeshua did not reach the community until the baby was six weeks old. When a young boy from the village ran in breathlessly to tell me of Jeshua's approach, I took the sleeping baby from my breast and handed her to Eena. Then I ran down the road to meet him. I stood for a while in the shade of a large tree trying to catch my breath. Jeshua and two companions came around the bend of the road and my heart skipped a beat at the sight of him. I ran the last few lengths to him and threw myself into his arms. He whispered my name and held me so tightly I could scarcely breathe. Those who had traveled with him went on to the village where a feast was being prepared in welcome.

I clung to Jeshua for some time sobbing, not yet willing to release him long enough to look carefully at him. Finally he pulled away a bit and I saw how very weary he was both in body and soul. He brushed the tears from my cheeks and smoothed the hair from my face.

"You look wonderful, Magdalene," he said, "a little older than when we parted. I see the child has arrived. Do we have a son or a daughter?"

"A daughter," I said with a smile. "I named her Sarah. I hope that meets with your approval?"

"That's a beautiful name. She is healthy, I take it?"

"Healthy and beautiful with the wisest eyes I have ever seen in an infant."

He took my hand in his.

"Let us go to her to tell her that our family is together at last."

The next few weeks were a combination of getting reacquainted and acclimated to our lives as a family, but mostly to our lives together without Sananda. His absence created a large emptiness within that Jeshua and I had great difficulty in filling at first. In time, we filled it with each other and the baby, but the first few months his absence was sorely felt. We each had access to him on the astral plane in meditation and in dreams, but it was not the same as his constant presence for three years. It must have been harder for Jeshua, for while I had the presence of my husband to hold to, he had become so used to sharing the body with Sananda that he mentioned to me once that he felt as though he was rattling around inside his body.

We began to make plans using the maps and information we had both brought with us and accumulated since our arrival. The Resurrection story spread as rapidly as wildfire in dry brush. Jeshua himself told us of his encounter with Saul of Tarsus on the road to Damascus shortly after his departure from Jerusalem. The guilt of all he had done to persecute Jeshua's followers resulted in Saul's blindness once he knew Jeshua's identity. Jeshua sent word to Peter of the blindness and we heard later that Peter had assisted in his care by giving Saul forgiveness and encouraging him to forgive himself. Though Saul changed his name to Paul, completely changed his life, and devoted it to traveling and speaking in Jeshua's name, he took too many liberties with the teachings and the stories and, we heard later, began insisting that Jeshua was a deity, the only actual son of God on earth. Jeshua was incensed, for the worship of him as a deity was so far removed from the intent of the teachings as to be laughable. It was thus, so soon after the Crucifixion, that the mission became splintered and perverted.

* * * * *

<u>*Sananda*</u>

Your (Magdalene's) resentment of me for the departure at the Ascension was very intense. You could not understand how I could dream of deserting you when you carried my child (mine and Jeshua's) in your womb. Oh, logically and intellectually you understood the need for me to return to spirit to oversee the many aspects of the mission from the "big picture" perspective, but the logic of your thinking did nothing to fill the ache of loneliness in your heart at my absence. The frail condition of Jeshua's body after the crucifixion made even the physical act of love unavailable to you for a long while. He stayed at Mount Carmel and was cared for by the Essenes for some months. That is why he was not present with you for the birth of our daughter, something you held against both he and I for the remainder of that lifetime. When you should have been nurtured, protected, and sheltered in the arms of the ones who loved you above all others, you were left to the tender mercies of those you traveled with from Palestine, your family members, Eena, and those in the entourage of Joseph. Mary, the mother, traveled with Joseph to the Holy Isles and visited with many of the learned men and women of the time. Joseph kept her from your side until Jeshua's return well after Sarah's birth. By that time she had resigned herself to your presence in Jeshua's life but she could never reconcile herself to the near worship status in which some held you and the baby.

You and Jeshua were apart for long amounts of time during the years of Sarah's growth and reconciled briefly for the conceptions of the sons for which he longed. You did not feel the intense love for them that you felt for Sarah because these babes had only an earthly father and were not borne of the love you and I and Jeshua had for one another as was she. You nurtured and cared for them, of course, but you were a little more distant with them than with our daughter. As the boys grew and were educated in the ways of the Jewish males of that time, they grew more like Jeshua and his brothers. They accepted the precepts of Jeshua's teachings as pronounced by the elders of the group that surrounded you and the small community. Your words were heard with reverence and awe by those who recalled the old days and remembered seeing the two of you (us) together teaching and spreading the words of light and love to all. But as the contemporaries of Jeshua met their fates at the hands of the Romans and other enemies throughout the empire, there were fewer who recalled the days of joy and light and the Days of Wonder, as the crucifixion and resurrection came to be called. As fewer remembered the days of your involvement in the work, the feeling began to grow that a woman, even one so learned and beloved of the Master as you, could not possibly have the ultimate grasp of the inner, hidden meanings of the teachings and messages that were given to Jeshua by God and passed to the inner circle of disciples. This feeling was encouraged by Peter, due to his jealousy of you and by Paul, due to his ignorance of your true role in the story, and spread throughout their various teachings and travels. James, let me point out, never said a word against you but his followers also questioned the wisdom of Jeshua allowing you the freedom to sit among the apostles and listen to the teachings. Little did they know that I would have had it no other way. I knew the precious little time that we were to have together and I wanted to be separated from you as infrequently as possible. As it turned out, the separations were much more than we planned and the precious time was cut shorter than we anticipated by the plots of those who wished to rid Jeshua of you and your influence. The plots and subterfuges that worked against you both were unknown to you until the very end. You had suspicions but no proof of the plots and conspiracy.

* * * * *

Chapter 24

All the while I was raising children and sharing the teachings with any who came to hear, a battle of sorts was being fought for the honor of being the one to lead Jeshua's followers to the Light of God. James took over the work in Jerusalem after Jeshua and I fled the area. He and Peter, then Paul, fought for the dominion of the new church. James felt he was the logical one to lead since he was of the bloodline. Peter felt he should lead because he was the apostle upon whom Jeshua supposedly conferred the power to "bind on earth as in heaven". Paul felt that his intellectual prowess and his encounter with Jeshua on the road to Damascus meant that Jeshua singled him out to lead all the churches and to make Jeshua's godly status an issue.

The truth is that Jeshua chose none of these. He just wanted the words to be carried. He cared not for any hierarchy that was set up and fought against any attempt to make him any kind of a god. People could not understand how a simple man could have the power that Jeshua demonstrated. They could not accept the truth of their own divine origins and the divine spark within and invented stories about Jeshua's divinity to give him the stature they needed to have in order to accept the authority of his words.

They all rallied around Jeshua for a time after he joined me and Sarah. They all wanted to make him the son of God on earth and to headquarter the church where we were. They visualized the beginnings of a Holy Empire, Jews ruling as they were meant by God to do. When Jeshua laughed at their grand schemes they were flabbergasted. They were still expecting the Messiah to have a palace and all the trappings of the King of the Jews. Even when he grew older and frailer they harped at him to establish something to leave behind. At this he would smile at Sarah and her children and our sons.

"I have a great legacy," he would say. "I leave behind the great joy I have found in my family."

I would smile and take his hand, then reach up to stroke his cheek and urge him to tell those gathered one of the many stories for which he was known. Even then the plan for preserving and protecting the descendants was forming in the minds of the faithful. Jeshua and I had no interest in their plots and plans for we knew the truth of what awaited us once we were done with the physical life.

We often got word of Paul's comings and goings. I was told that his intent was good but that he was very opinionated and thought too highly of his ability to decipher the truth of Jeshua's words. The "vision" on the road to Damascus that day gave him the "authority" with some to speak in Jeshua's stead. In reality, he had no idea that it was really Jeshua in the flesh that he met on the road that day. The two had a lengthy philosophical discussion before Jeshua turned the tables and accused Paul of persecuting him. The blindness that Peter cured led Paul to many insights, but when it came to Jeshua's teachings he missed the boat. He got the words right and thought he knew the meaning. Then he tried to deify Jeshua.

Yes, Jeshua was a Messiah, but all have the potential to become Messiahs, carriers of the Christ energy. The exclusive club in which people place him is not exclusive. This is the point Paul really missed. He explained the philosophy of the day, the place of women in the church, but that concerned him very little. He essentially encouraged the church to silence half the population and encouraged celibacy of the deacons and priests to solve a temporary problem.

Jeshua never asked nor expected celibacy, not being celibate himself, nor did he wish to silence the voices of the women or deny them power, but because Paul spoke with the voice of authority and invoked Jeshua's name whenever possible, those who heard assumed they were the wishes of Jeshua. Jeshua respected me, not just as his wife and the mother of his children, but as a woman with a brain, intellect, and wisdom. I had my say in everything. I was fortunate enough to have had an education that few women had and was quite opinionated, but I had the teachings of Jeshua and Sananda to back up those opinions.

I traveled with Jeshua and the group. I taught. I helped and assisted the women of the group to open to the possibilities that the life they knew was not all there was. I helped open the eyes of the men to the realization that the minds of women were not the empty things that some believed. I could not abide the unfairness in a situation and that was only one of the things that made me furious about Paul's words and attitudes and the unfairness of his decisions. He made it appear that the women involved in the scandals he spoke to were the instigators when in reality the men did the pursuing. Jeshua emphasized the importance of communing with God in the heart and soul rather than in a building but Paul deified him and insisted that the only way to commune with God the Father was through Jeshua and in a building designated for that purpose.

No, I never cared for the words of Paul and the way he changed the direction and focus of the teachings. I tried to believe that his intent was the survival of the early churches, but I suspected that his real intent may have been his own survival.

Meanwhile, I was ever hopeful of the day that Sananda would keep his promise to me when the time came and return for me, reach out his hand and take me home to spirit.

* * * * *

It is nice to know that in spirit time has no meaning. Even the longest of physical lives is but a blink in the mind of God. To one in a physical body, however, time drags endlessly when you are waiting for the return to spirit. The years passed as years do. Jeshua spent much time traveling the world and teaching the love of God to all who were open to listen. James stayed in Jerusalem for a time until the political climate took him as it did many of those who followed Jeshua. He established the church in Jerusalem that became well entrenched in the eastern part of the world.

Peter preached Jeshua's words as he understood them and established a following throughout the Mediterranean. His emphasis on the Jewish rules of diet and circumcision did not set well with those of other ethnic backgrounds. Paul recognized this and focused less on the old traditions and more on his interpretation of Jeshua's words as heard from those who had known Jeshua and heard him speak. Although his intentions may have been good, the message did not relay the intent of Jeshua's words.

Please do not think that I became a pillar of goodness and a shining example of the way for all to live. I lived each day to the fullest. I laughed often, cried on occasion, embraced frequently, and told everyone who would listen about the extraordinary times of Jeshua and the group. The only one with whom I shared the full story was Sarah when she was old enough to understand about Sananda and the merging of his soul with Jeshua's.

Chapter 25

Jeshua and I were seldom together during Sarah's childhood. His travels kept him away for long periods of time. Although he always professed his deep and abiding love for me, the pain of our days together in Jerusalem was too difficult to overcome. Our shared memories were too private to be discussed with anyone else and too painful to talk of between us. Living apart became a way of life and Sarah and I contented ourselves with the times he came to visit. One day in late spring when Sarah was nearing her twenty-third birthday, Jeshua came home for the last time.

He looked more weary than ever and I could tell that in spite of his relative good health, the drudgery of constant travel was beginning to take its toll. Sarah was delighted to have her father home for good and her three little ones were thrilled to have their grandfather to play with and to tell them stories about the exotic places he had visited and the interesting people he had met. He did his best to settle into a life at home with his family but the years came between us and we found the chasm too wide to bridge. We lived in quiet contentment for the most part enjoying the days with Sarah and the babies, Evenings were filled with frequent visitors, friends and neighbors who were pleased to have Jeshua home and who longed for his teachings and wisdom.

As he grew more frail, I tried to make him get more rest and to take better care of himself, but he was so accustomed to overdoing when it came to the work that he found it nearly impossible to slow down. He began making very short trips to neighboring villages for the day but was always back by nightfall so I would not worry.

One afternoon a young boy ran into the yard calling my name. When I calmed him and he caught his breath, he told me that Jeshua had collapsed at his home down the road and was asking for me. Sarah left the children with a neighbor and we set off to find Jeshua. We had scarcely set off when we met a small group coming our way with Jeshua on a litter.

I went to Jeshua's side and took his hand.

"Do not make a fuss, Magdalene," he said weakly. "I am just a little tired today. I'll be fine tomorrow."

I smiled at him and stepped aside as the men made their way to our home and put Jeshua to bed. Sarah and I got him settled and comfortable and left him napping. As I walked into the gathering room Eena and Simon came in and Eena ran to me crying. She threw her arms around me and sobbed on my shoulder.

"How is he, Magdalene?" she asked when she had composed herself. "Simon was with him when he collapsed and said Jeshua sent him for me. What is wrong with him?"

"I think the years may have finally caught up with him, Magdalene," Simon said quietly. "He spoke to me this morning about how weary he is and how he longs for the time to return to spirit. He seemed to be delirious for a moment and was speaking to the air, to someone he called Sananda."

Simon reached out to steady me as my knees threatened to buckle. My stomach clenched and my hands began to shake. Sarah made me sit down and brought me a cup of cool water. I looked up at her and saw the same stricken look on her face that she must have seen on mine. He had not spoken openly about Sananda to anyone but me and Sarah and it had been years since we had heard the name spoken. We both feared what this meant.

I spoke quietly to Simon and asked that he send word to any of the group still living who might be close enough to travel here in time to say goodbye to Jeshua, for I knew that he was ready to return home to spirit. Good friends are those who step in and take over when needed and, luckily, Jeshua and I had friends like that in our small community. When my conscious mind realized what was going to happen, I must have denied it on the surface. Other than asking Simon to send for those of the group, I did not refer to the possibility of Jeshua passing on. I continued to go about my daily life as though untouched by the reality I soon would face.

Jeshua lay sleeping much of the time. Occasionally he rallied enough to drink some clear soup or heated wine, but I could see him wasting away almost minute by minute. It seemed to me that his spirit was escaping little by little leaving only the physical husk behind. Sarah and Eena were with him nearly constantly urging him to swallow one more spoonful of broth or take another sip of water. They bathed his face in cool water and encouraged him to share the happier memories of our lives together. Sarah heard stories from Eena and Jeshua that she had never heard before.

It was wonderful to hear her giggling at Eena's version of Jeshua overturning the tables of the Temple moneychangers and the near escape they all had from the Temple guards. She told of the baptism of James and Jeshua, the day that Sananda merged with Jeshua. "Though I did not know at the time exactly what had occurred," she said looking at me, "I saw the light and heard the voice and knew that something extraordinary had happened. Sananda spoke to me when Jeshua collapsed, Magdalene. He said to hurry to you both and to be here for you and Sarah. He said that you would explain it all to me in time."

I fought back tears and nodded. I did not trust myself to speak. Sananda was still looking out for me just as he had promised so long ago on the hill beneath the full moon.

Slowly the days passed without Jeshua regaining strength. He continued to linger, perhaps waiting for the group to gather one more time so he could say goodbye. While they sat with him, Eena and Sarah embroidered little white flowers on the blanket that lay at the foot of the bed. The red blanket was one of the gifts that Jeshua brought back from his travels to the east and was made of the softest wool. He told me that the color reminded him of our passion and the softness of my hair lying against his skin.

As the days passed into summer, members of the group

arrived one or two at a time to pay their respects to Jeshua. They entered the room with smiles and came out in tears, embracing me, some of them weeping openly. Most of the group had been scattered to the winds, many fallen victim to the Romans. Peter and Paul and James were dead along with numerous others, each sharing the teachings as they understood them to their last breaths.

Most of the family was gone, too. Mary, Jeshua's mother, had died some years before, though she lived long enough to see Sarah grown and wed to Phillip. We never grew to be friends, which I regretted, but were civil to one another for the sake of Jeshua and the family. She never understood me or accepted that my ways were different than her own. She taught Sarah many things about running a household that I had little patience for and in this way became more content with her life in the end. For this I was glad.

The summer heat passed and autumn was approaching when Jeshua took a turn for the worse. For months he had refused to leave his bed except to change the linen. Though he did enjoy having the grandchildren come to visit with him. Now the weakness was worse and he could no longer raise his head from the pillow. Simon called softly to Sarah from the bedroom door and told her to call the family quickly. I stood before the door for a long moment dreading to enter. I had lived through Jeshua dying once. Must I endure this a second time? Suddenly Lord Michael's voice came to me and I felt his powerful presence to my right.

"You can do this, Magdalene," he said. "You brought Jeshua back to life with your strength and your command. You gave up your will to the Father so his good could be done. It is now his will that Jeshua go home to spirit. Look within your heart, my dear. You cannot deny that this is also Jeshua's will and his need. He again waits your word. Send him home, Magdalene."

I nodded and straightened my resolve. I placed my hand on the door and gently pushed it open. Sarah sat on the far side of the bed holding Jeshua's hand. Eena sat on the near side but vacated the spot for me and went to stand with Simon at the foot of the bed. Phillip stood beside Sarah with his hands on her shoulders to give her strength.

I sat on the side of the bed and took Jeshua's hand. It felt light and his skin had become thin and fragile. He opened his eyes and smiled weakly at me. "Magdalene," he whispered.

I leaned forward and said softly, "Jeshua, my husband. You have and always will be the love of my life. Thank you for choosing me to be the one to accompany you on this great adventure we have had together. We have had grand and glorious happiness, sadness and despair. But always we have come through it together knowing we were fulfilling God's will for us. But you are weary, my love, and you have done more than anyone could have asked of you. You have fulfilled all of the Father's wishes for this life and you have willingly laid down your very life in order that the truth of his love will be seen and known in every heart. You have done all that it is possible for any soul to do in one short physical life."

"You have friends who love and respect you, and a multitude of those whose lives have changed for eternity through your words and your love for them. You have a family who adores you and love you above all others. You have accomplished so much, my love, so much for which to be proud."

He reached up weakly and caressed my cheek, gently wiping away my tears.

"Don't cry, dearest. I will watch over you always," he said softly.

"I know you will, Jeshua. I love you and always will. But the time has come for you to go home, my love. As I once called you back to life, now I release you so you may return to the arms of the Father from whence we all come. Take with you all the love that I bear for you. Go home, my love, my husband. It is time."

"She is right, Jeshua," said a voice.

I looked up in shock. There stood Sananda smiling down at Jeshua.

"She is usually right," whispered Jeshua with a smile. "I love you, Magdalene. Forgive me."

"My love, there is nothing to forgive." I said and squeezed his hand. I leaned over and kissed his cheek. "Go home, my darling. I will be along presently."

Jeshua closed his eyes and took a final breath. Sananda reached for his hand and drew Jeshua's spirit from his body. Suddenly Jeshua's spirit was beside Sananda and they were embracing and laughing. They both turned to me and each kissed my cheek.

"Goodbye, Magdalene," said Jeshua.

"Magdalene, I will always be with you. Do not forget." Sananda caressed my cheek and smiled. Then he and Jeshua faded from sight.

I caught my breath in a sob. "No," I called. "Take me with you. Do not leave me!" I sat with my arms folded around me and sobbed. Eena came to hold me and Phillip enfolded Sarah in his arms.

Sarah came to my side and knelt beside me. She took my hands in hers.

"Mother," she said, "I saw them. I saw Sananda come to take Father home. I saw them!"

I looked at her and saw that it was so. It had not been a delusion of my grieving mind's making; it was real. Sarah had seen it, too. I should have felt better, I should have been relieved that Sananda had kept his promise to return for Jeshua. If he returned for Jeshua, he would return for me. But seeing them together in spirit did not help me, in fact it made it worse. Here I was, still in the physical, still left behind to deal with the consequences just like after the crucifixion, just like after Sananda's departure. Now I was alone. They were both gone, gone forever this time. There would be no resurrection, no miraculous return to life. Nothing but an empty body to put in the ground. Yes, I could rejoice that Jeshua had been released from the body which had served him so well for so many years. I could rejoice that he was now in spirit where he would no longer have pain or suffering…or me.

At that thought, something within me snapped. I stood up and announced, "I am going out."

"But Magdalene," said Eena," we must wash and anoint his body and prepare it for burial,"

"Go ahead." I said. "I have already done that. I washed and anointed him when they laid his body in my lap fresh from the cross. I did my duty to him then when there was none but his uncle and friend to help, when his trusted followers fled to preserve their own lives. I have done this one time. I will not do this again!"

Sarah and Eena looked stunned, for I rarely raised my voice in anger. Simon touched my shoulder gently.

"We will take care of him and call you when all is prepared. Go breathe in the fresh air."

I walked straight out the door and went outside where I found a group who had heard Jeshua was dying and gathered. I pushed my way past them and climbed the hill in back of the house to the big oak tree. There I sat down and leaned against the massive trunk and sobbed. I cried for my loss of Jeshua and Sananda. I cried for all the years spent in silence with Jeshua in which we did not even speak about the good days with Sananda, for the reminder of his absence was more than we could bear. I cried for the futility of all we had done. I spoke to Jeshua of all our accomplishments, but what had we really done? Only spoken to a few people about the love of God, the Father, and the truth of life in spirit. We had taught the kingdom within but how many really understood the meaning of those words? How many knew to look within to the soul rather than outwardly to the designs of man and religion?

The more I thought of those years the angrier I became with the whole situation. I cried, I vented my fury. I railed at Jeshua, at Sananda, even at God. Through it all, I could feel their presence trying to comfort me, but I refused to acknowledge them or to be comforted. Finally, I cried myself to sleep in the soft grass beneath the tree and dreamed of being held gently and strongly in Lord Michael's arms, his wings wrapped protectively around me.

An hour or two later, Sarah came to find me. She woke me gently and we shared hugs and tears.

"Come, Mother," she said. "All is in readiness and the others are waiting for us."

We made our way to the place which had been prepared for Jeshua's burial. I watched silently as his body was placed in the ground and covered. When it was done, several of those present spoke, telling stories of their time with Jeshua or repeating some of his sayings. When they asked me to speak, I could not.

One by one, they paid their respects and went to the house until I stood alone in the gathering darkness beside Jeshua's grave. As if to mock me, a full moon rose over the hill and shone its light on me. Again, a full moon to light my loss. It was more than I could bear. I walked into the house and told Eena that I did not want to be disturbed, went to my room, and shut and locked the door. The bed had been stripped of linen but the red blanket with its white embroidered flowers was draped over a chair. I pulled it around me and curled up on the floor and cried myself to sleep.

Morning's light found me still huddled on the floor. The tears were replaced with a rage so intense it hurt my heart. I screamed and cried and cursed even the two whom I loved above all others. Their very names were no longer words of love but the reminder of their abandonment of me. Twice Sananda had abandoned me to the physical for the world of spirit where I was denied his embrace, his touch. Jeshua, too, was withheld from me, first by injury and then by death. I was tired of being magnanimous, tired of being the one to take care of others and being left to my own devices. Resentments I had not known I carried all bubbled up and demanded to be acknowledged and dealt with. And so I cried and yelled and beat my fists against the walls of my self-imposed prison until they were bloodied.

"How could you leave me alone in this place? You promised you would never leave me! How dare you leave me here by myself!"

Then one morning, Sarah's voice penetrated the dark

and hazy fog of my grief as she begged me through her tears to open the door and remember her grief, too. I pulled myself together as best I could and unlocked the door. Sarah threw it open and flung herself into my arms.

"Thank goodness, Mother. I was beginning to fear that I had lost both of you!" Sarah cried and refused to let me go for a long moment. Then she wrinkled her nose. "You've been in here for nearly a week. Come and eat then wash and change your clothes while I air out your room."

I reluctantly left my room for an hour and was glad to feel clean and fed again.

The next three weeks passed slowly. Sarah and Eena threatened to break down the door unless I came out daily to wash up and eat. Gradually every day was a little easier. I was able to let go most of my anger and resentments knowing that all works as God intends, and who was I to tell God he had made a wrong choice?

In time I returned to my work. I taught Jeshua's words, especially to the women and children. I told them of Jeshua's great respect for women and his love for children and the way he delighted in playing with them and telling stories. Doing the work I was meant to do cleared my heart and soul and soon I was feeling better and was able to finally let go of my anger towards Jeshua and Sananda. As soon as that happened, they both came to me in my dreams. We had wonderful discussions about the days gone past and the days to come. They advised me on the teachings and helped me to see new perspectives and gain new insights into the teachings. Neither one referred to my lengthy temper tantrum or chastised me in any way, but I know they were relieved that I had finally regained by sanity and stability.

Chapter 26

One thing became clear to me as time went on. I was going to be in the physical for quite a while longer and it was important to reach as many people as I could with Jeshua's teachings. I did not want to travel the world as he had done. I was content to stay in my own house and feel the live of my family and friends. It was Sarah who first suggested that I put her father's teachings in writing.

"There are a lot of people spreading what they call his teachings," she pointed out one day," but you know how false they are. Some are so far removed from the intent as to be laughable. Why don't you write his words and teachings so they won't be lost to the world? If you worked on this every day, it shouldn't take too long, and look what a remarkable gift you would leave the world!"

Eena and Simon agreed, and as they were the only two left (at least in the area) who had heard Jeshua speak, we three sat down daily to recall and record Jeshua's teachings and his stories. I was unsure as to the extent of our personal lives to include, but Sarah reminded me that at my passing, there would be no one left with any of those memories.

"Do it for me and my children, please, Mother," she begged. "I know the information is very personal, but you and Father and Sananda had a unique time together and a unique love story. It would be a shame if that story was lost forever."

So despite my misgivings, I wrote our story. I told about the locket, our marriage, the baptism and the coming of Sananda. I wrote with many tears the story of the crucifixion and the miracle of Jeshua's return to us. I relived the heartbreak of Sananda's return to spirit and our journey across the sea to our new home.

When Sarah read of the locket, she asked to see it. I pulled from beneath my gown and let her look at it. When she found the hidden clasp and the locket opened, she exclaimed in delight at the coil of braided hair still resting within the locket.

"It's still here!" she said. "May I have the locket, Mother? It will be my way to remember you both and the love you shared."

"When I go home to spirit the locket will be yours. Until then, it will rest beside my heart where it has been every day since your Father sent it to me when I was sixteen. This is the first time it has been opened since he placed the braid in it on the night of our wedding."

Sarah closed the locket and handed it back to me. As I slipped the chain over my head she smiled.

"I will be happy to have the locket to wear, "she said, "but please do not let that day come for a long while."

* * * * *

Day by day I worked on writing all the memories of my days with Jeshua, the good, the bad, and the chaotic. As I remembered and wrote of the simple tasks, the tender moments, and the touching events, I noticed that my heart and soul were healing. No longer did I harbor resentments against either Jeshua or Sananda. I no longer held them personally responsible for my feelings of abandonment. I began to understand the higher truths of what we had done together and saw for perhaps the first time what far reaching consequences the teaching could have in the world.

Simon was able to procure for me some of the storage jars used by the Essene communities in which to store the completed manuscripts. When all the writing was done, Sarah and I had a little ceremony as we sealed the manuscripts into the jars. Phillip dug a small chamber into the side of the hill next to the house where we had a root cellar and kept wine and root vegetables in the cool earth. We made sure the jars were sealed against the dampness so the writings would be preserved for many years.

"How will we know when the time is right to open the jars?" Sarah asked one day.

"Sarah, I think you and I and perhaps even your grandchildren will all be in spirit by the time the writings again see the light of day. God will see to it that the right person will find the jars at the time the world is in most need of them. We must trust in his wisdom."

I labored over the right way to begin the collection of writings. One just doesn't jump in to a story. Jeshua taught me that you need to introduce the story and its characters in a gentle way so they will live in the minds of the reader or listener. And so I took a fresh sheet of parchment and carefully began…

"I remember Palestine…"

Chapter 27

The day finally came when I knew that I had done all I could to preserve the story of Jeshua and me. I had written the story and sealed the jars. I had taught and trained younger men and women who would carry on the work after me. In truth, I was tired. Jeshua had been gone more than twenty years when I became ill with a sickness that I couldn't seem to shake. To be honest, I did not want to recover. I wanted to go home to spirit, to rejoin Jeshua and Sananda, to once again feel their love for me and to lay down the many burdens that this life had piled upon me.

Sarah was concerned, of course, but she had Phillip and her children and grandchildren. It was hard to realize that my daughter and Jeshua's was now an old woman herself. She sat by my bedside and talked to me of the family's activities. As she brought me up to date on the travels of the new teachers, the newest churches, and the latest in stories attributed to Jeshua or myself, it occurred to me that all the years of passion about the work were gone. It was no longer my responsibility. I could do nothing further. I had no reason to linger here other than Sarah, and she would not long remain after me.

Eena and Simon were gone to spirit. They were the last of those who had witnessed the truth of Jeshua and me. Some of the stories being perpetuated were glaringly false, others were merely slight exaggerations. It was all out of my hands now. I was more than ready to leave behind this lifetime behind.

As the spring afternoon lengthened, Sarah woke me and took my hand.

"Mother, can you eat something? I have a fresh pot of your favorite lamb soup with spring vegetables. Are you hungry?"

I shook my head weakly. “No, Sarah. I am too tired to eat. I think the time has come for me to go home.”

“I will not ask you to stay any longer. I know how tired you are, Mother. I will just sit here with you if I may.”

I nodded and closed my eyes. Then I heard it.

“Still sleeping, Magdalene? Come, Beloved. We have things to do and places to go.”

I opened my eyes and saw Sananda standing beside me, smiling at Sarah, who looked at him with her mouth open in astonishment.

“Lord Sananda!” she said. “You have returned for her!”

“Of course, my child. We always keep our promises.” Jeshua’s voice came loud and clear from where he stood next to Sarah. He placed a hand on her shoulder. “Thank you for taking such good care of her for us.” He leaned over and placed a kiss on her head. “When the time comes, we will return for you, also.”

Sarah squeezed my hand gently and leaned over to kiss my cheek.

“Goodbye, Mother,” she whispered.

Sananda stretched forth his hand and smiled at me.

“Come, Beloved. It is time to go.”

I stepped easily from my body and felt the exhilaration of being freed from the heavy physical body I had worn so long. I looked into Sananda’s eyes and smiled. I looked at Sarah who watched us with tears in her eyes and smiled at her, then linked arms with both Sananda and Jeshua.

“I’ll bet you she scolds us for waiting so long to come for her,” said Jeshua with a grin.

“You are probably right,” Sananda replied. “She always was impatient.”

We laughed together as we moved away. I glanced back once to see Sarah slipping the chain of the locket around her neck.

Then we made our way to the group that had assembled to greet us led by Archangel Michael. I laughed as he gathered me up in an embrace and enfolded me in his wings.

I was truly home.

Epilogue

In the year 2015, in the wine country of France, Pierre and Marcus worked together to expand the wine cellar of Marcus' house. Built into the side of the hill, the cellar had been there for as long as anyone could remember. The constant and cool temperature was perfect for storing the local wine that was famous the world over. A wine collector and connoisseur, Marcus had recently acquired the contents of a cellar belonging to a deceased collector before word got out about its availability. Now space was the issue and the reason for expanding the existing cellar.

Marcus and Pierre stood in the doorway with a glass of Merlot watching the two workmen as they dug more earth from the back of the cellar. They were about to set a date for golf when one of the workmen called excitedly to them.

"Monsieurs! Come see, quickly!"

As Marcus peered around the workman, he saw a stone wall behind the wall of the cellar.

"It looks like it has been here a very long time. Shall we leave it or continue digging?"

"Continue digging. It's probably just the side wall of an older cellar," said Marcus.

The workman continued and soon the stones were removed revealing an opening to a small room. They continued removing the stones until a larger opening was made so that the smaller of the two could enter.

"What do you see?" asked Pierre.

"Just some old storage jars," the workman replied.

"Bring them out. They may contain something of value," instructed Marcus.

Pierre gasped when he saw the first jar.

"Marcus! These are antiquities! Look at the seals! We

must be very careful with these."

Marcus and Pierre each carried a jar while the workmen followed with two others. Marcus led the way into his study and placed the jar carefully on the library table. The others placed their jars carefully beside it.

"What do you suppose is in them?" asked one of the workmen.

"I have no idea," replied Marcus. "Let's see."

He took a penknife from his pocket and carefully slit the seal on the smaller jar. He carefully lifted the lid and peered inside.

"What do you see?" asked Pierre.

"Some kind of parchment or papyrus, it looks like. I am going to see if I can remove one of the sheets."

"Be very careful," cautioned Pierre. "It could be a priceless relic of some kind."

Marcus carefully coaxed the innermost sheet from the rolled sheaf of parchment and gingerly laid it on the table before him.

"Can you make out the writing? It looks like some kind of foreign language to me."

Marcus took a magnifying glass from a desk drawer and peered closely ay the writing.

"I think this may be Latin. I seem to recognize some of the letters."

"Let me see," said Pierre. "I took Latin at university."

Marcus handed Pierre the magnifying glass and moved aside. Pierre looked closely and began to slowly read aloud.

"I remember Palestine…"